John Henton Carter

Duck creek ballads

John Henton Carter
Duck creek ballads
ISBN/EAN: 9783743377172
Manufactured in Europe, USA, Canada, Australia, Japa
Cover: Foto ©ninafisch / pixelio.de

Manufactured and distributed by brebook publishing software (www.brebook.com)

John Henton Carter

Duck creek ballads

Duck Creek Ballads

BY

JOHN HENTON CARTER
(COMMODORE ROLLINGPIN)

AUTHOR OF "THOMAS RUTHERTON," ETC.

NEW YORK
H. C. NIXON
117 NASSAU ST.

TO MY SONS,

W. N. AND E. B. CARTER.

SIMPLE rhymes is all they air,
    Writ about the Southwes' whcre
Folks talk plain an' som'times swear.

Livin' clos' to natur' they
Alus take the sho'tes' way
To say what they've got to say.

Dialec' its called by some
Easte'n folks that chence to come
Out here lookin' fur a home.

But it savors o' the s'il
An' the forests an' the wil'
Flowers that cultivation sp'il.

An' the people un'erstan'
Ev'ry accent spoken an'
Cling to it on ev'ry han'

On its sho's the cottonwood,
Dreamin' in its mossy hood,
Casts its shadder on the flood.

An' the rustic lovers glide
In the twilight side by side,
Happy that the worl's so wide.

An' the birds air singin' there,
Notes that can't be heard elsewhere,
Voicin' natur' unaware.

Keep yer cultur, ef ye will,
It's a purty thing, but still
Let me hear the whipperwill

Warblin' nigh the everglade,
Where no teacher yit hez strayed
'Cept the one that music made.

Simple rhymes o' simple things
Jes a nes' o' mutterings,
Hatched out an' given wings.

CONTENTS.

	PAGE.
THE OLD HOUSE ON THE CREEK,	1
THE POET'S WIFE,	6
HOW JIM BECAME GOVERNOR,	8
WHY THEY GAVE,	11
THEM GOOD OL' BOATIN' DAYS,	13
COBBLER BROWN,	17
THE EDITOR'S REWARD,	20
DOT POY,	23
ARISTOCRACY PLACE, NO THOROUGHFARE,	25
THE MATE OF THE BLUE GOOSE,	28
LIFE,	31
WHY DAVE WILLIAMS SWORE OFF,	32
THE ETERNAL LAW,	35
THE CAPTAIN'S STORY,	37
THE LITTLE SHOE,	39
AN ODE TO SPRING,	41
THE LAND OF THE SANDWICH,	43
THE MEMBER FROM OZARK,	47
ROCK ALONG,	49
MOTHER'S ALUS HED HER WAY,	51
THE DUSTY SEASON,	53

CONTENTS.

	PAGE.
The Dying Striker,	56
The Pilot's Story,	59
Mattie Stephenson,	63
The Ghost of the Mary Ann,	65
Decoration Day,	67
The Summer Solstice,	70
The Vision,	73
The Mutineer,	75
The Train Fiend,	78
What Broke Up the Church at Sorby,	79
To My Books,	84
Knox's Landing, Mississippi,	87
What the Clock Said,	92
Zeke Slabsides,	94
Pickett's Post Office,	100
The Mysterious Suicide,	103
He Wanted to be Counted In,	107
The Member from Cohoes,	111
The Mystified Traveller,	113
Linguistic Lore,	116
Fit with Grant,	118
Atonement,	120
The True Creed,	122
Watering the Stocks,	123
The Martyr,	126
The Wabash Ranger,	128
Tobe Gray,	130

	PAGE.
DRAW ONE,	132
THE MATE OF THE MARIA,	133
TO A SOLDIER OF THE UNION,	136
THE CHECOT ELECTION,	138
THE PAUPER,	143
DEACON BARKER'S PHILOSOPHY,	144
THE RAID OF THE HOPPER,	146
CAPTAIN BOB RILEY,	151
AN ODE TO AUTUMN,	154
THE WHISKY RING,	156
THE NOBLE RED MAN,	159
THE MYSTERY OF KERRY PATCH,	162
NO LUCK IN PRAYER,	167
CIVIL RIGHTS IN SHREVEPORT,	169
THE HERO OF NATCHEZ BEND,	172
THE APPLE MAID,	175
THE COUNTY FAIR,	179
CHRISTMAS EVE,	180
THE SAD FATE OF PETER JONES,	181
MISSISSIPPI SMITHERS,	185
A MUD THEORY,	187
SANDY POSEY,	188
THE NEW AMAZONS,	190
SANDY THOMPSON'S STEERS,	192
THE UNRECONSTRUCTED,	195
THE WHITE COLLAR LINE,	199
BLANNERHASSETT'S,	202

Duck Creek Ballads.

THE OLD HOUSE ON THE CREEK.

I'VE hed a hankerin' o' late, to jes pick up an' go
A visitin' aroun' amongst the fo'ks I ust to know.
I've studied on it till I find I'm gittin' real homesick
To set my eyes onct more upon the ol' house on the crick.

The 'roma o' that cellar is a clingin' to me yit,
An' to think o' that b'iled cider, makes me too dry to spit.
Why I seem to taste the ginger, an' hear the poker sizz,
An' share with Uncle Dan agin, that temp'rence drink o' his.

I want to see who's livin' an' who's married an'
　　who's dead,
Ef all the young fo'ks kep' their word, an' done
　　jes what they said.
What boys hev writ their names upon the scroll
　　o' fame, an' who
Accomplished all in after life, that they set out
　　to do.

What become o' Hiram Mueller, that hed the
　　freckled face,
An' could never learn his lessons; is he on the
　　ol' place?
In the footsteps o' his father, an' ez close fisted
　　too?
I reckon ef he is that he is purty well to do.

I'd like to see the spring agin, at which we ust
　　to drink,
An' set down by it on the grass an' hev a good
　　long think
About the youthful faces it onct mirrored like a
　　. glass,
An' how the worl's been treatin' em sence all this
　　come to pass.

Who married Becky Wilkinson, they ust to call
    the belle,
An' how she 's passed the time away? I want
    to hear her tell.
Hez her "path been strewn with roses, an' her
    skies been alus bright,"
Ez I writ in her album, in the best hand I could
    write?

Maybe the birds air singin now, the songs they
    ust to sing,
When apple-blossoms were abroad, an' all the
    sweets o' spring
Were rompin' in the medders an' the woods an'
    garden where
We ust to stroll together in the quiet evenin' air.

I'd like to visit mother's grave, neglected all
    these years,
An' ef nobody wuz aroun', maybe to shed some
    tears;
Leastwise ef they should start, I 'low, I've only
    this to say,
I wouldn't try to stop em, but let natur' hev her
    way.

I wonder ef the terrapin, on which I cut my name,
Is browsin' in the clover yit, an' lookin' jes
    the same,
Er ef his gait's a gittin' slow, his eyes a little dim,
An' age that gins to pester me, hez also come to
    him?

Ef brother Smiley's preachin' still down at the
    "Horner" Mill,
An' every other week er so, comes up to Jenner's
    Hill
To tell 'em all about the broad, an' o' the
    narrer way,
An' how to read their titles clear, an' sheep that
    went astray?

An' after chu'ch is out ef he goes home with
    Uncle Dan
To eat a dinner that's got up on the ol' country
    plan?
Ef this is so I hope that they'll remember when
    I'm there,
To not furget the circumstance, an set me up a
    chair.

I'll 'gree to set all afternoon an' hear em argify,
About the scriptur's an' the crowns, awaitin' 'em on high.
Jes to set eyes onct more upon a hunk o' pumkin bread;
An' other luxuries on which in early youth I fed.

So I guess I'll wait no longer, but jes pick up an' go
A visitin' aroun' amongst the fo'ks I ust to know.
I've studied on it till I find I'm gittin real homesick
To set my eyes onct more upon the ol' house on the crick.

THE POET'S WIFE.

THE Poet's wife hath pensive face,
    And sighs,"O, dearest, why thus chase
A phantom? 'Tis a hopeless race.

'Twere better for us both by far,
That you should stand behind a pa'r
Of mules upon a bob-tailed car,

Than thus to burn the midnight oil,
In one unceasing round of toil,
That fails to make the kettle boil;

Or start a peanut stand, or take
To any calling; only shake
This one, that surely takes the cake

For a precar'ous livelihood;
Far better turn to sawing wood,
Or rid the crossings of the mud."

But lo! the poet "strikes it;" when
She sheds her pensive face, and then
Becomes her dear, old self again.

And never since hath uttered word
Of phantoms chased, or hopes deferred,
And not a breath is ever heard

Of sawing wood, or peanut stand,
Or wrestling with the muddy land,
Or bob-tail car, or aught she planned.

But free at last from care and strife,
She layeth hold of social life
And poses as the Poet's wife.

HOW JIM BECAME GOVERNOR.

Ez to the Guv'ner, sir, why Jim an' me
    Were boys together, workin' on a farm
Till well nigh grown. Then fur variety
We tuk to browsin' 'roun' permiskusly,
Gittin' thicker an' thicker, from the start,
Till it seemed ez ef we couldn't live 'part.

At last we tho't we'd take a little rest,
    An' visit 'roun' am'ung our ol' time friends,
An' show our boughten cloth's, fur we were dress'd
An' rigged in fin'ry o' the very best.
An' ez fur munney, why we made it fly
Ez ef it growed on trees a standin' nigh.

One day we stopped to see ol' Deacon Brown,
    Ez owned the big farm over on the run—
All bottom lan' an' lots o'other groun',
An' the fines' gal ez wuz ever 'roun'
These here parts. Waal Jim fell in love on sight
An set up courtin' her that very night.

Then he chenged his ways an' refused to drink,
    An' settled down to edecate hisse'f,
An' bought some books, he said to help him think
An' staid up readin' till his eyes 'ould blink,
They 'lowed she wouldn't hev him, but she did
An' tuk the chences that the futur' hid.

Waal, lovers promises hev wings, you know,
    An' Jim's, they soon spread their's an' flew away,
An' then he tuk to carryin' on so
Her kin folks 'lowed she'd better let him go.
But woman like, she never would gin in
She'd throwed herse'f away in marryin'.

But she fell off, ez ef she might be crossed
    In love, an' then her rosy cheeks growed pale.
He seem'd to gain more strength'n she'd lost
'Thout ever stoppin' fur to count the cost,
Till the doctor said that she wuz nigh gone,
Then he got scared an' went to takin' on,

An' stayed at home an' set up day an' night,
    An' nussed the baby an' tuk care o' her,
An' all a sudunt got awf'ly polite.
Then everybody 'lowed that Jim wuz white;
An' when she hed it cris'ened at the chu'ch,
He were't a man to be left in the lu'ch.

So he jined to an' went to leadin' prayer,
   Wuz made a Deacon, an' then a trustee,
An' every meetin' held, why he wuz there,
An' alus ready to do his full share;
An' so you see, the critter riz an' riz,
Till everythin' you see 'round here's his.

An' the cap-sheaf he's puttin's on to-night
   At his 'naugral, an' all the quality
Air pourin' to the house from left an' right,
In carriages, an' proud o' the invite.
An there'll be dancin' an' the band 'ill play
"Dixie," "Hail to the Chief," an' "Happy Day."

An' now, you know his hist'ry sir, altho'
   I might keep on a ta'kin' by the hour,
Fur we wuz equ'ls twenty years ago,
An' might be yit, but drink is drink you know—
An' so that's how Jim become the Guv'ner,
An' sir, he owes it ev'ry bit to her.

WHY THEY GAVE.

"WHY do you give?" the matron said
    To the housemaid standing near,
"Your acts encourage, I'm afraid,
    These beggars to gather here,
Your charity is ill bestowed
    On these mendicants, I fear."

Awhile the maiden stood demure,
    But made answer presently,
"I give," she said, "unto the poor
    That come to the house each day,
As one acquainted with the pangs
    Which arouse our sympathy."

"Why do you give?" a stern man said,
    To a Christian at his side;
"'Tis best that each should earn his bread,
    Than thus to be supplied.
You nurture idleness, I fear,
    Which, I hold, should be decried."

"I give," replied the holy man,
    As he grasped the other's hand,
"Unto the needy all I can,
    Because, as I understand,
The Master makes imperative
    Such an act in His command."

"Why do you give ?" another asked,
    Of a man of lands and gold,
"Your avarice is poorly masked
    By this flimsy cloak, I hold;
The miser's visage ill becomes
    The hand of generous mold."

"I give," he answers with a sigh,
    While great tears his eyes bedim,
"Because of a son that's never nigh,
    But roams to the wide world's rim,
In hopes that someone in his need
    May be moved to give to him."

THEM GOOD OL' BOATIN' DAYS.

AN aged man of feeble step, whose hair and
beard were gray,
Betook him to the river front, just at the close
of day.
He cast his eyes about as if their waning sight
to test,
Then resting them upon the stream, these senti-
ments expressed:

"Alas! I am a relic of the pre-railroadic age,
An' come out hyar occasion'ly my sorrer to as-
suage,
By callin' up them good ol' times o' forty years
ago
When I piloted the Elephant, from 'Orleans ter
Cairo.

When the river wuz the unly route a trav'ler could take,
An' folks didn't bet on ho'ses, but the time a boat could make;
When pine-knots hed a value that hez not been known o' late,
An' no oleaginous thing wuz safe among the freight.

When berths wuz alus open ter them as wished ter ship,
An' every man renewed his paint, on each succeedin' trip;
When a pilot had standin' in the best society,
An' a capta'n wuz the envy o' the community.

When a game wuz alus waitin' ter while away the time,
An' the bark o' the revolver not an unfamil'ar chime,
When the grub wuz the fines': an' the liquor in the bar
Sech as ter make an angel wish ter pay a vis't thar.

When the papers puffed the boatman, from
  captain ter the *chef*,
An' a man could eat his breakfas', an' read
  about his se'f;
When wimin' wuzn't runnin' arter city dudes
  an' sech,
But threw thar bate at river men ez' bout the
  fines' catch.

When they cl'ared away the cabin, at evenin'
  fur a dence,
An' every man ez' knowed a step wuz gev a
  white man's chence,
While the barber played the fiddle 'n the porter
  the banjo,
An' the steward called the figers, 'swing pard-
  ners, do ce do!'

But moughty few I 'low air lef' o' that air noble
  ban';
They're planted all along the sho' er sleeping in
  the san'
Jest waitin' till ol' uncle Gabe shell soun' the
  final call,
When they'll rise'n lead the dancin' at the res-
  urrection ball.''

He ceased and as he vanished a halo spanned his brow,
It seemed angelic whisperings were familiar to him now,
And as if answering the same, he murmured, "O ye Let,
I'll be thar with my pardner an' waltz in the fust set."

COBBLER BROWN.

The happiest man of all the town,
Is the cobbler Ebenezer Brown;
Who sits on his bench from day to day,
And stitches and trims and pegs away;
Humming a rhyme in an undertone,
The burden of which no ear has known:
  "I've a wife I love and children three,
  And few so poor as to envy me,
  Yet the bread of toil is ever sweet,
  And I'm thankful we've enough to eat."

His leather apron is soiled and worn,
And his meagre "kit" has served its turn.
And the floor is bare and the windows, too,
But the morning sun comes streaming through
And casts a halo about his hair,
Till it seems a saint has stole in there.
  "I've a wife I love and children three,
  And few so poor as to envy me,
  Yet the bread of toil is ever sweet,
  And I'm thankful we've enough to eat."

In a wooden chair his Lena sits,
And in sweet contentment sews or knits.
While the baby with a cast off shoe,
Is trying to cut it's "toofys frew."
And two rosy boys are standing near
Watching the pegs as they disappear.
> "I've a wife I love and children three,
> And few so poor as to envy me,
> Yet the bread of toil is ever sweet,
> And I'm thankful we've enough to eat."

No thought has he of to-morrow's store,
Nor vain regrets for what is o'er,
But pursues his honest task each day,
And at evening smokes his pipe of clay;
Yet no millionaire in all the town
Is happier than the Cobbler Brown.
> "I've a wife I love and children three,
> And few so poor as to envy me,
> Yet the bread of toil is ever sweet,
> And I'm thankful we've enough to eat."

Long may he cherish the simple rhyme,
And when age shall come as 't must in time,
And strength shall fail and his eyes grow dim,
May some one cheerfully toil for him.
And the halo of life's setting sun
Encompass the brow of this saintly one.

"I've a wife I love and children three,
And few so poor as to envy me,
Yet the bread of toil is ever sweet,
And I'm thankful we've enough to eat."

THE EDITOR'S REWARD.

A journalist from Duck Creek, of the ancient Bourbon school,
Whose chief ambition is to yearn for Democratic rule,
With beaming brow, and sprightly gait, stepped from an early train,
And hastening to the White House, proceeded to explain:

"My father was a Democrat, likewise my grandsire, too,
And all my readers know I print a paper that's true blue.
I hold man's highest aim should be to propagate the creed,
And sow and till with patient hand the monticello seed.

"I helped to run you in, you know, just eight long
 years ago,
And toiled with others that you might succeed
 yourself, also.
And after having skipped a term, you're seated
 · in the chair,
I think that I may safely say I helped to put
 you there.

"Your picture hangs upon my wall, with that of
 Mrs. C.
And baby Ruth, and every week, I freely puff
 all three.
I've named a boy, also two girls, in honor of the
 same,
And feel that I have started them upon the road
 to fame.

"But now my paper, like my wife, is needing a
 new dress,
Not that I think of them the more, nor of the
 children less.
So I've come on with signatures, a little place
 to seek——"
And drawing forth his parchment, he wisely
 ceased to speak.

The Presidential eye was thrown upon the
    mighty list.
"You'll have to take your turn," he said, "in
    the official grist."
And then he tossed the document upon a pile
    near by,
So large it filled the capitol, and rose into the
    sky.

They parted and the editor sought the outgoing
    train,
And on his pass was landed safely at his home
    again,
Where he still does noble battle against his
    party's foes,
But his paper and his family are wearing their
    old clothes.

DOT POY.

"COOM here, mine leetle Peterkin,
    My bromisin' yung zun,
Und dell me efry ding you gin
    'Bout dot great Vashington.
Vot for dey praise him oop so high?"
    "Because he couldn't tell a lie."

"Yah, dot vas so, mine leetle shent,
    Vat odor dings you know
'Bout dot great man vas Bresident
    Von hund'ed years ago?
Coom, shpeak him oudt, I vants to see"—
    "The hatchet and the cherry-tree."

"Dere nefer vas a poy dot vay
    Dem shesnuts all to learn;
He pees der Bresident soom day
    Ven it cooms to his durn.
Whose fader vas he? dell dot to me."
    "The father of his country."

"Ha! Ha! Ha! Ha!—vell, I'll be plowed,
    I vants to roll der floor,
Sooch happiness vas nefer knowed
    To coom to me before.
Dot poy he make me feel so broud
    I vants to shout mineself oudt loud."

ARISTOCRACY PLACE, NO THOROUGHFARE.

A DUET.

CROESUS:

"I'm a *ton* and reside in a place you can't match,
There's a gate at each end, and no string to the latch,
    For exclusiveness nothing can with it compare.
    Aristocracy Place, no thoroughfare,
        No thoroughfare,
        No thoroughfare,
    Aristocracy Place, no thoroughfare."

TOILER:

"Perhaps 'tis Utopia, the pure ideal state,
Can environment make one the master of fate?
    Do the cares of the world never enter in there?
    Aristocracy Place, no thoroughfare,
        No thoroughfare,
        No thoroughfare,
    Aristocracy Place, no thoroughfare."

CROESUS:

"Your emotions arise from your necessities,
My position assured I've no such vagaries,
    Which accounts for my reticent *nonchalant* air—
    Aristocracy Place, no thoroughfare,
        No thoroughfare,
        No thoroughfare,
    Aristocracy Place, no thoroughfare."

TOILER:

"Can riches bring peace to the care-burdened soul?
Or surfeit inspiration ? Then what is the goal ?
    Is it the life of elegant leisure you share ?
    Aristocracy Place, no thoroughfare,
        No thoroughfare,
        No thoroughfare,
    Aristocracy Place, no thoroughfare."

CROESUS:

"O! your logic belongs to the sour grape brand,
'Tis the bird in the bush, not the bird in the hand.
    You'll reform it, no doubt, when you've more *savoir
        faire.*
    Aristocracy Place, no thoroughfare,
        No thoroughfare,
        No thoroughfare,
    Aristocracy Place, no thoroughfare."

TOILER:

" Then *sauve qui peut* is the creed you would teach,
(Save himself who can and not each other save each).
　Ah! The seal of your tribe's on the masonry there:
　Aristocracy Place, no thoroughfare,
　　　　No thoroughfare,
　　　　No thoroughfare,
　Aristocracy Place, no thoroughfare."

CROESUS:

" I've no time to be bandying words here with you,
Life at best is but brief, and no one can have two,
　So let him reap who can the full lion's share—
　Aristocracy Place, no thoroughfare,
　　　　No thoroughfare,
　　　　No thoroughfare,
　Aristocracy Place, no thoroughfare."

TOILER:

"O! then be it my lot to remain ever poor,
That my faith may increase, as I toil and endure,
　For I envy you not your fine mansion in there—
　Aristocracy Place, no thoroughfare,
　　　　No thoroughfare,
　　　　No thoroughfare,
　Aristocracy Place, no thoroughfare."

THE MATE OF THE BLUE GOOSE.

The boat hed made a landin'
Fur a mule that wuz standin'
    On the rise o' groun' jes above the slip,
But in spite o' their bluffin'
An' tail-twistin' an' cuffin',
    He didn't seem inclined to make the trip.

He wuz a sorry critter,
O' com'on country litter—
    Big-headed, shaggy, cockle-bur'ed an' mean;
An' jes sech a quadrupid
Ye'd reckon wuz too stupid
    To feed hisse'f ef turned out on the green.

"Come now, le's hev this mule in,"
Said the Mate, "an' no foolin';
    We kent stay here a monkeyin' this way,"
When Si Wiggins said, "come, git——"
Waal, I'm sorry to admit
    That Sirus ain't been heard o' sence that day.

Then Brophy took occasion
To observe that moral 'suasion
    Sometimes proved more effective than hard blows.
But deaf to all entreaty
An' gatherin' his feet he
    Brought Brophy's brief career to a close.

The rousters now were bilin'
An' fur a fight were spilin'—
    'Cep them ez hed been sent to kingum come,
An' interduced heroic
Treatment on that air stoic
    By poundin' him with rails an' bo'lders some.

But they kep' on expirin',
Fur that mule wuz untirin'
    In puttin' heads on all 'at did assail,
Ontil there come a stillness,
An' the Mate felt a chillness,
    Fur he alone wuz lef' to tell the tale.

Then he cast on that critter
A look ye might call bitter,
    An' made remarks that I'll not put in rhyme.
Suthin' 'bout ez 't wuz the rule
O' a com'on kentry mule
    To be alus keepin' boats ahin' their time.

Then the dus' it riz an' flew
Till it shut em both from view,
    An' fur a spell they gouged an' punched 'way,
Till the racket wuz mistuk
Fur an earthquake that hed shuk
    The setttement surroundin' there that day.

The *Blue Goose* went puffin' 'long
Ez ef nuthin' hed gone wrong,
    An' lookin' out fur other stock an' freight,
Leavin' that air stub'orn mule
Hol'in back ez wuz his rule,
    An' determined that he wouldn't immigrate.

LIFE.

Two vessels in mid-ocean meet,
  And "ship ahoy," each other greet:
"Oh! whence and whither—sail so fleet?"

"I hail from out the silence there"—
  Each gazing back with solemn air—
"And hie, alas! I know not where."

When one came walking on the sea,
"Lo, I reveal all mystery,
  He finds a port who follows me."

WHY DAVE WILLIAMS SWORE OFF.

No boys, I've quit
An' done with it;
An' hereafter don't furgit
When ye'r' drinkin' to pass me—
I've tackled my las' whisky.

That's how I stan'
On this thing, an'
Fact is I've been a dif'rent man
Ever sence that Chrismas night
We went home from Frazier's tight.

You know I'd been
Dead sober then
Fur more'n a year, an' so when
Belle catched sight o' me she fell
Over in a faintin' spell.

I staggered to
The house an' threw
Myse'f down—that's all I knew
Till mornin' an' woke to find
She wuz still out o' her mind,

An' on the floor
Sence the night afore,
Handsomer 'an when she wore
Her bridal dress, an' gin to me
The keepin' o' her destiny.

I lay her on
The bed ez one
With life 'bout already gone,
An' nu'sed her all alone till she
Opened her eyes an' looked at me.

An' sech a look,
It almos' tuk
My breath, ez I stood an' shuk;
Fur I knowed all her mis'ry
Wuz caused by that on'ry spree.

An' I said, "Belle,
Ef ye'll git well,
I'll never do it 'gin." I tell
Ye, her an' drink couldn't agree,
An' she's my wife. No, thank ye!

The act might kill
Her, boys, keep still—
Go in yerselves ef ye will,
But ez fur David Williams, he
Hez tackled his last whisky.

THE ETERNAL LAW.

A rose upon a summer day,
Called to the billows plaintively,
"I languish for thy cooling spray."

To which the ocean made reply:
"I fill with moisture yonder sky;
Turned thitherward thy longing eye."

A vessel, sadly tempest tossed,
Goes down and all aboard are lost,
Though pious hands in prayer are crossed.

When from the lightning's forked tongue,
Re-echoing the stars among—
"Man perished thus when time was young."

A toiler uttereth his moan,
"Alas! my every hope hath flown,
I sow where harvests are unknown."

When, lo! a brooklet, rippling by,
Cries in exultant melody,
"There are green fields beneath the sky."

Two kindred souls are joined as one
In "holy rites"—the years go on,
And sorrow comes between anon.

"Lord, teach my feeble lips to pray—"
One cries in anguish—"lead the way."
The other perished in its clay.

THE CAPTAIN'S STORY.

I run the boat mysel'f, an' you see
We ust to think it a mystery,
Till the truth come out, an' then we knew
'Twuz human natur' through an' through.

Aunt Martha Goode wuz our chambermaid—
Not much of a heroine, I'm 'fraid
You'll find but little in sech to praise,
It's a cur'ous story, anyways.

Fur whether sweepin' er in the suds,
Er ironin' er a mendin' duds,
When the whistle blew fur Notre Dame,
Out on the fo'castle Martha came.

With a pu's' o' money in her hand,
Which she gev to some one on the land,
Then back agin to her work she'd skip,
To repeat the same thing the next trip.

She must hev a frien' out there, some said,
Others 'lowed her wrong about the head,
So things went on till we come to call
It Aunt Martha's whim, an' furgot 't all.

But one evenin', she sent fur me—
"Capt'n, I'm a goin' to die," says she,
An handin' me her money she said:
"Please send it to him when I am dead."

Tell him it ez frum his frien' that knew
His mother, an' to be good an' true.
I've written here his address an' name —
It's Albert Saunders o' Notre Dame.

That is the story o' Martha Goode,
How she sacrificed her motherhood,
Rather 'an it should be known that he,
Her son, descended from sech as she.

Ez fur the boy, he kin hold his own
With the best o 'em, an' more is known.
He's married now, an' settled down
Ez Judge Saunders—you'll excuse the town.

THE LITTLE SHOE.

'Tis but a little russet shoe,
    Quite stringless and forlorn,
And void of sole; and wrinkled, too,
    And sadly bent and torn,
As if the childish feet had sought
    Life's tumult at its morn.

"An ornament, an ornament,"
    Dear loving Grandma cries
In tones of sudden merriment,
    Denoting glad surprise,
While placing it upon my desk
    Where pen and paper lies.

"I found it in the closet there,
    Among his other toys,"
She spoke as when some memory rare
    Arouses vanquished joys,
And a sweet vision of the past
    The yielding soul employs.

It holds its place a welcome guest,
    As fleeting years go by,
And lo! the little one that blessed
    Our home is ever nigh,
To cheer us in our lonely hours,
    In tones that cannot die.

AN ODE TO SPRING.

To sing o' gentle spring may be all right
Fur other latitudes, but don't indite
Sech nonsence 'bout the wild an' wooly west.
Fur a more vig'rous spring suits her the best.

O' all the seasons o' the rollin' year,
Spring is the one that's most upon its ear.
Out on a reg'lar tare from fust to last —
Talk 'bout its bein' gentle, lemme ast:

Is a cow gentle that you tell to "hist,"
An' kicks the bucket over about twiced
Afore you start to milkin' her, an' when
You say, "so, Bossy, so," an' try again,

An' find she wont, but to your great surprise,
Plants both her feet 'bout where your supper lies,
An' goes right on a eatin' o' your hay?
But let me put in another way.

Imagin' fur a minute you hev thrown
Your lamps upon a rip roaring cyclone
That's p'inted fur your shanty an' you jes
Crawl in the underground hole with the res',

An' wait till it hez passed and then you see
Your house an' barn a keepin' company
With that same gentle zepher, that's the spring
O' which a weste'n poet hez to sing.

THE LAND OF THE SANDWICH.

Since the good Kalakua,
Of the Kingdom of Hawaii
Put aside his regal sceptre, they've been having quite a pull
As to who shall rule Owhyhee,
Maui, Oahu, Malokia,
Kaui, Lauia, Niihau, Kahoolaui, as the sovereign mogul.

O, isles of the Pacific,
Where Kilauea burns terrific,
'Neath her heaven-piercing peak, with its hoary crown of snow,
And the lavas hieroglyphic,
Invites men scientific
To ponder over forces that are potent down below,

Tell us Mauna Helekala,
Will thy fire be ever fallow?
Shall thy burning eye be quenched in an ever
during night?
Will you need our oil or tallow,
To allume your coast so shallow,
Or our live electric wire, which we claim is out
of sight?

Is there money in stock raising?
Are your mountains built for grazing?
And in brief, have you resources to maintain a
sovereign state?
Have you ceased forever praising
The shark God? Are your ways in
Keeping with our system, or is monarchy your
fate?

How about the festive Sandwich?
Does it flourish? Is the brand which
Adorns our lines of travel, of the vintage you most prize?
Have you widows that are big—rich,
And handsome maidens and sich?
And what of their complexion and the color of their eyes?

Answer by return of steamer,
For our eagle is a screamer,
And he's out "for a roll," on his skirmishes, you bet;
And we yet may have a prem'er,
That will see his way clear
To send old Uncle Samuel's fleet and lift you from the wet.

THE MEMBER FROM OZARK.

He kem ter these hyar parts a few years ago,
A straunger without any sort o' a show,
No money or credit ter start him in biz,
But pluck, game an' sech like war em'nently his.

So gittin' his grip on a thousand er less,
He purchased fo'thwith an ol' cylinder press,
An' openin' an office, immed'ately he
Commenced fur ter print a rip-snortin' daily.

The Court House an' Council he carried by storm,
With an article headed: "sweeping reform",
Which closed by declarin', he meant ter pursue
A course that would bring all corruption ter view.

The printin' he got by a *coup 'd 'etat*,
An' fur a brief time he suspended the law,
Commandin' the ol' city dads ter keep still
While he groun' out some light frum *his* gospel
    mill.

The news that he printed war some ter behold,
He'd bury a critter afore he war cold,
An spin out an epitaph forty lines long
'Fore his victim 'ould know thar' war anything
  wrong.

Perlitical meetin's war his very best holt,
An' ye jes orter 've seen *him* conductin' a bolt,
When the thing warn't goin' a'cordin' ter Hoyle
An' a nigger got in er a chap truly lo'al.

I tell ye, ol' man, he war pisen on 'em,
An' night an' again he'd go off on a bum,
Thought nothin' o' makin' a twenty mile tramp
Jes ter git ter throw shell in a radical camp.

But he's a law maker now in Jef'son Cit',
An' warms like a statesman a seat in the pit.
Got his lamps on the White House—the Pres'-
  dent's cha'r,
Waal 'f ever he starts h'll wont keep him from
  thar.

But I s'pose everything is the will o' the Lord,
An' our member is jes takin' in his reward—
Though I 'low he's more faith in healthy green-
    backs,
Than he hez in the morals taught in yer tracks.

ROCK ALONG.

Should fortune frown upon your path,
   Press on with might and main,
Each victory gained, the hero hath
   More strength to fight again.
So face life's daily battles with a heart that's
   brave and strong.
Rock along, Rock along,
     Rock
         along.

If you're in love, and she you seek
   To be your life-long mate,
Informs you hers is not the cheek
   On which you'll vegetate,
Don't sound your troubles to the world as if
   you were a gong.
Rock along, Rock along,
     Rock
         along.

There never was a maid so fair,
    That could not find a match,
You've heard about the fish out there,
    Also about the catch—
So don't proclaim yourself a bell and ring out
      your "ding-dong."
Rock along, Rock along,
      Rock
          along.

And if at times your lot is hard,
    Your blessings very few,
If others play the winning card,
    While scarce a trump hold you,
Don't fancy that you're fated to endure a lasting
      wrong.
Rock along, Rock along,
      Rock
          along.

MOTHER'S ALUS HED HER WAY.

"Mother alus hez her way,
  Hev to ast *her*," pap would say;
When a circus come to town,
  Er some other show wuz' roun',
We were hankerin' to see
But were sho't o' currency.
Fur she alus kep' the pu's'
Ez a so't o' family trus',
An' when anything wuz done
That would trespass on the fun'
That the ta xes hed to pay,
Mother alus had her way.

Seemed ez she wuz bo'n to do
An' act jes ez she ust to.
Nothin' studied er put on,
Jes the same to every one.
Kind an' gracious ez a queen,
Smilin' on us so serene,
That her presence seemed to fill
An' illume the house. Her will
Firmly fixed on things above—
Leadin' us with filial love,
Through the twilight to the day—
Mother alus hed her way.

Faults we hed an' many, too,
But she never looked us through,
Ef she did she only saw
What wuz perfec', not the flaw.
Ez that night when Dan an' me
Come home from the huskin' bee,
Staggerin' to the house so tight,
Could n't 'stinguish black from white.
An' she put us both to bed,
Not a word wuz ever said,
But when she kneeled down to pray—
Mother alus hed her way.

Sittin' in her chair I see
Mother ez she ust to be,
With her yarn upon her lap,
Knittin' socks fur me an' pap,
Sister Sue an' brother Dan,
An' the baby Debby Ann.
Thinkin an' a plannin', too
What's the bes' fur us to do.
Though she's dead these twenty years,
Everything the same appears,
See her now ez plain ez day—
Mother's hevin' still her way.

THE DUSTY SEASON.

Of all the ills which vex mankind,
    There's none that is so trying
As stepping out to always find
    This "terra firma" flying.
There's nothing we can say is ours;
    Our gardens can't be trusted,
For yesterday I planted flowers,
    And they got up and dusted.

My lettuce, too, and cabbage failed,
    The radishes are dying,
And, goodness, how the madam railed
    To see the beds a-flying!
"Look here," said she, "at this vile room!
    I'm perfectly disgusted."
"My dear," said I, "just get a broom;"
    And she got up and dusted.

The doctor came to feel the pulse
    Of Nell, who had the fever.
"I have no fear for the results,"
    Said he, "I'll soon relieve her;
Her peck of dirt she's ate this week,
    And never once mistrusted;
Some purer climate let her seek."
    And she got up and dusted.

For weeks we battled with the foe,
    Who gained upon us daily;
The Steinway's ruined, the clock won't go,
    The canary sings less gaily;
The dog looked like a walking farm
    Of vegetation busted,
And, fearing still more serious harm,
    Why, he got up and dusted.

"Go for the Mayor," said I to John,
 "Be quick and get about;
Tell him to send a posse on
　With spades to dig us out."
But blind with dirt, he struck the fence,
　And his proboscis busted,
Then, striking a two forty hence,
　Why, he got up and dusted.

Above I saw the lightning flash,
　And heard the distant thunder;
Anon, another deafening crash,
　Which said, "All stand from under."
Then quickly came the welcome rain—
　Before any one mistrusted—
And here I would remark again,
　That we got up and dusted.

THE DYING STRIKER.

Mother, draw aside the curtain,
    Let me see the light once more,
And the calmly flowing river
    That we loved in days of yore:

Ere the sordid hand of progress
    Smote its banks with cinders dire,
And illumed the peaceful valley
    With its all-consuming fire.

Progress! surely is it progress
    That the common mass should toil
In the glow of molten metal
    Till their very souls recoil?

Falling in the awful ordeal,
    And in silence perishing,
That some vain, ambitious creature
    Should become an "iron king!"

THE DYING STRIKER.

I was one among the many,
    Following the scriptural plan,
Seeking bread by honest labor,
    Loving well my fellow-man;

Thought it nobler far to suffer
    Than by trickery to climb,
Trusting in the pretty stories
    That are taught in prose and rhyme.

Well, perhaps I was mistaken;
    It was but an idle dream,
A delusion fondly cherished,
    Not at all what it would seem.

Yet perchance the toiling millions
    Coming after us may say
That their burden was made lighter
    By the men who fell to-day.

Mother, come and close the curtain,
    All repining is in vain;
Alien hands are in possession,
    And the strike has failed again.

'Tis the oft repeated story:
    And the old unequal fight;
Yet some time in the future
    God will set our cause aright.

THE PILOT'S STORY.

B'lieve in sperits? Waal I 'low
I'm leanin' that way anyhow,
Ever sence the Vivian
Bu'nt an' sunk in Bunch's Ben',
During the big overflow
Back in seventy. Eh, O!

Ez to how I come to change
My min' you may think it strange,
But facts air stubborn things, an' we
Can't go back on what we see.
I'll tell you how't come about
Ef you've time to hear me out.

All aroun' wuz pitchy dark,
An I could't see a mark
Er a thing to hold 'er on,
Fur the shore an' stream were one,
An' the rain come peltin' down
Till it 'pear'd the boat 'would foun'.

I could unly let 'er drift
With the current; makin' shift
To catch a glim'se o' suthin when
It lightened. We hed been
Floatin' this way fur a spell
When I heard the watchman yell

"Fire, Fire, land er quick!"
Then somebody gin to kick
In the stateroom doo's an' shout;
"Git up here an' hurry out;
Put yer life preservers on,
An' be lively or ye're gone."

Sech a scene of sufferin'
I never wan' to see agin,
Women screamed an' chil'en cried—
Men grew pale 'n holler-eyed
An' speechless; like they were dumb,
An 't seemed the jedgment day'd come.

Twenty year er more its been
Sence we lost the Vivian,
Yit I never pass the place
But I'm forced agin to face
All the dismal scene around
An' the hun'er'n people drowned.

An when stars air overhead
An' the fog begins to spread
On the water an' the land,
Then I see 'em hand in hand,
Ghostly white an' thin ez air,
Here an' there an' everywhere.

Playin' sort of hide an' seek—
Young an' frisky, old an' weak—
Glidin' where the shadders play
'Long the sho' an' then away
To where the bayou tunnels through
The cottonwoods DeSoto knew.

Waitin fur the trumpet's call
That shell summons one an' all
To that region far away
Where a never endin' day
Lights the river an' the shore,
An disasters come no more.

MATTIE STEPHENSON*.

So young, so fair, her life was all too brief,
    Yet gauge we not her worth by length of days,
But rather by our own enduring grief,
      And sweet remembrance and unceasing praise,
      And the recurring pleasure that we find
    In giving her sweet story to mankind.

Alone she watched until the moon went down,
    Bathing the feverish brow with tender care;
Again the faithful Howard, in his round
    At early dawn, pauses to find her there;
      But not the cheerful maid of yesterday.
      Ah! would there were no sadder word to say.

---

* The Heroine of the Memphis Epidemic, 1870.

Sleeps she in unknown grave in future time,
   O'er which the modest ivy creeps unsung?
No! let the monumental marble climb,
   And her sweet name unto the world be flung.
      Time hath no nobler heroine revealed
      Than she who fell with those she could not shield.

THE GHOST OF THE MARY ANN.

"Water hez ghosts ez well as lan',"
  The pilot said, "you un'erstan',
  I seen one climb that air jackstaff
  Every night an' look 'fore an' af',
  An' stan' my watch ez though that he
  Wuz pilotin' instead o' me.

  But it ain't thar now—don't be skeered—
  Been sometime sence it disappeared,
  An 't wont come back hyar I allow
  A roostin' 'roun' this hyar ol' skow.
  I'll tell you how it come to go,
  Ez I reckon you'd like to know.

  I stood it fur a month er more
  When one night says I, go a shore,
  The Mary Ann can't hol' us both.
  I wuz riled'n mought a used an oath;
  But there it set till my watch wuz through
  An' Jo wuz called, when away it flew.

Four o'clock I wuz up agin
An' at the wheel—when durn my skin!
Thar set the ghost on the night-hawk;
In front o' me—I gev a squawk—
But it only turned 'roun' an 'peard
To think 'at it hed got me skeered.

This was too much, says I, call Jo
To hol'er till I go below,
An I loaded up my fusee,
That never yit went back on me –
An' drawin' a bead on its head,
I cracked away—that ghost wuz dead."

* * * * * *

They'd stuffed a suit of the captain's clothes,
An' every night the same they rose
Up by a cord and that was what
The pilot saw and what he shot:
But ever since the old man boasts
To the passengers he's death on ghosts.

DECORATION DAY.

Dec'ration Day, eh? Waal, it never kems roun',
But I think o' a critter ez lef' this town—
Been gone, lemme see, fur this thirty odd year,
I'll tell ye how 't war, mum, ef ye'd like ter hear.

Wilkins Bowers war his name,—kem, now, don't
    git skeered,
Been a moughty long time sence he dis'peared;
Why thar ain't a gal ez is spreadin' them flowers
Ez ever heard tell o' this same Wilkins Bowers.

He warn't much on love, but he captured one gal
Though sheer cussedness, ez the folks ustter tell;
Fur he never dun nothin' but loaf an spree,
An' why she lived with him war a mystery.

Waal, her cheeks growed pale, an' she kept
    takin' on,
Ez women'll do, an' war purty nigh gone;
Fur men when they're a drinkin' can't symp-
    perthize,
An' tears air a weakness that some fo'ks despise.

But soon the war kem on, an' he jined the ranks,
An' the people o' the neighborhood gev thanks
Fur the takin' o' this on'ry Bowers away.
Why, I remember it ez though it war ter day.

'Twar a summer mornin', an' the Colonel said,
"Fo'ard, brigade, march!" an' then, with a
    steady tread,
They waltzed 'way ter the front down in Ten-
    nessee.
Please keep yer seat thar, Mum, an' don't star'
    at me.

Then the san'tary folks kem aroun' with grub
An' clothin' fur the woman and her little cub,
An' the neighbors allowed how ol' Uncle Sam
War a far better pervider than her ol' man.

An' she thinks me dead, an' every blessed year
Kems hyar with the res' jes ter drap a tear
On the soldier's graves an' keep their memories
 green,
Jes like a woman (but oh! how she is agin'.)

No, I never kin tell her, better far that she
Worship her hero ez dead than 'gin live with me.
An' that young man's yer son, Mum—Waal yes,
 I knowed Bowers,
But the crowd's a moving' on, go an' spread yer
 flowers.

THE SUMMER SOLSTICE.

My love is where sea breezes blow,
   And I am keeping house alone—
   'Tis somewhat novel I must own,
But very pleasant, don't you know!

I trust the change will do her good,
   I feel that it is helping me—
   I haven't had such liberty
Since putting off my bach'lorhood.

What care I now for ten o'clock?
   There's none to say, "John, come to bed."
   I sit and read and nod my head,
And rousing read again and rock.

The sun may climb the vaulted sky
   And kiss the dew from off the flowers,
   I take my ease, nor count the hours
Nor days as they go flitting by.

THE SUMMER SOLSTICE.

Of breakfast I partake at nine,
    And rarely dine till 6 P. M.,
    I'm taking my meals out "pro tem,"
No cooking done at home in mine.

For I have drawn the curtains down,
    And closed up the vestibule,
    And sit up-stairs where it is cool—
Ostensibly I'm out of town.

And so complete is the device,
    That none who are disposed to call,
    Suspect that I am watching all,
And playing it upon them nice.

The gas fiend stops and stares about,
    And hums "Eh! eh! they're all away,
    I'll charge 'em up for every day—
The company shall be nothin' out."

No more the dust's wild freaks to tame,
    The sprinkling cart's sh-i-sh, sh-i-sh is heard,
    Nor has it from the stable stirred—
They'll send the bill in, all the same.

Anon, the tanned old harvester
   His sickle rests upon the gate,
   He says, "I'll hang aroun' an' wait,
It can't be long till they air yer."

The huckster, too, goes creeping by;
   With sullen look and muffled voice,
   He feebly calls out "hyar's yer choice
Apples! 'taters! melons! cel'ry."

The tinker cries, "tinware to mend,"
   Though carrying his furnace cold—
   He rarely lights it, I am told,
He's keeping up his fly-time end.

The book agent unbends his load
   Of moral works in monthly parts,
   Confronts the closed-up house and starts
With the remark, "Waal, I'll be blowed!"

And so each day they come and go,
   And keep a watch for our return,
   And sweat beneath the sun and burn—
I'm sorry for them, don't you know.

THE VISION.

While musing, how the years had flown,
    With scarce a trace of victory,
And garlands I had wove were prone
    To wither in obscurity.
A vision rose of noble mien,
    And sang to harp, "dismiss thy fears;
Let not ungarnered hopes restrain
    The efforts of the coming years."

Then all was changed, a stately hall
    Rose in the incandescent space;
"He cometh now," aloud they call,
    While joy illumes each anxious face.
And as he spoke, Promethean fire
    Leaped from his lips, and lo! again
The vision smote the trembling lyre:
    "Familiar he with toil and pain."

A study, wherein works of Art
　　And bric-a-brac and books abound,
Came next in view and stood apart,
　　The envy of the world around.
And seated in his easy chair,
　　A famous author plies his pen—
"He, too, has wrestled with despair;"
　　The vision sang, "take heart again."

THE MUTINEER.

Thar wuz a man that run on the Mississippi ez mate,
He wuz'nt much on book larnin' an' he didn't set up late
Postin' hisse'f on hist'ry an' civerlization,
But when it kem to sportin' news he beat all creation;
An' ef ye went to his bunk ye wuz jes sure to fin'
All the leadin' papers in that air partic'ler line.

He wuz on his mussle somewhat, which is an ol' complaint
With them Mississippi river boatmen—thar's few that aint—
An' he could git mor' work out o' his men on b'iled beans
An' hard tack, 'an any mate from St. Louis ter Orleans.
His voice, it war jes immence an' kem up outer his boots,
An' 'specially when he yelled "kem, git thar, ye d—d galoots."

One day he said to a rous'about who hed on his
    back
A four-bushel sack o' co'n—a big load, but it's
    a fact,
How that he 'lowed that air gait o' his'n wuzn't
    jes up to time,
When they got inter a dispute that I'll not put
    in rhyme,
But I'll state no mor' co'n wuz carried on that
    boat that day,
Fur all the crew wuz occypied in seein' 'em hev
    fa'r play.

They shook things up lively fur more'n three
    quarters o' an hour,
An' rammed thar heads right inter 'bout a dozen
    ber'ls o' flour,
An' the grain 'n' things that wuz spilt 'roun' the
    lower deck
Made it look like the boat hed struck a snag an'
    gone to wreck,
An' this here mate who never yit hed los' a
    single fight
Saw that his chences fur kemin' out second bes'
    war bright.

So when he foun' he couldn't git 'way with that
    rous'about,
He begun to git oneasy an' cussed an' hollered
    out:
"Say is yu-uns all gwine to stan' 'roun' this boat
    all day an' see
This inscrbor-nation? I say thar, stop this here
    mutiny!"
An' that is the moral that I hev been tryin' fur
    to paint,
When them mates lick a man, it's all right, an'
    when they don't, it aint.

THE TRAIN FIEND.

O! yes, he's there when you take your seat,
    And will go with you all the way,
Until your journey you do complete,
    If you're pointed for Canada.

He dumps his books promiscuously,
    And then vanishes through the door,
And now we will have a rest, you say,
    But there's where you're off on your lore.

In vain you plead that you cannot read,
    That you rarely indulge in fruit,
He knows there's truck on which you'll feed,
    And hustles for something to suit.

And when he closes his empty pack,
    And skips at the end of the run,
You may learn by your depleted sack
    Of the havoc that he has done.

WHAT BROKE UP THE CHURCH AT SORBY.

Thar's nothin' parfec' in this worl' is my ph'losophy,
An' we're about ez ap' ez not, ter bark up the wrong tree:
Fur things air alus happenin' that seem way out o' place,
An' ter a moral, thinkin' man, a scandalous disgrace.

What I am drivin' at is this: jes set down, thar's a cha'r—
An' I will do my level bes' ter make the whol' thing cl'ar,
Fur time hez dulled my memory, an' cu'bed my use o' speech,
An' many things I ust ter know, air now out o' my reach.

The craps war kemin' on right fine, the co'n war
    up knee high,
The wheat war ripenin' han'somely, so war the
    oats an' rye,
An everything war prosperin' jes ez the Lo'd
    hez said
It should be with the hones' fo'ks ez arn thar
    daily bread.

An' so his wo'd seemed jestified by everything
    aroun',
An' then ter make it mo'e complete, His grace it
    did aboun',
Fur while the farmer bushed his peas an' sot up
    his bean poles,
The pa'son war a prosperin', in rakin' in the souls.

Bassy Prather, he kem for'ard, an' so did
    Larfin Bill
Jones, an' all them scoffin' tanners frum over by
    the mill
On Eagle Crick; an' then thar war that wicked
    Sandy Moore,
Who hedn't been inside a chu'rh fur twenty
    year afore.

He kem up ter, an' 'lowed ez he'd throw up all
    his strife
An' gredges, an' the likes o' that, an' lead a
    dif'rent life,
An' when the meetin' it war out, we every one
    dispu'sed,
Fur Sorby, down on Hardon Crick, ter see 'em
    all immu'sed.

The Pa'son waded in the crick; the people
    gath'r'd roun',
An' stood whar an' uprooted tree hed riz a little
    moun',
But when he took a brother by the han' ter lead
    him out,
Ye'd a thought ol' Nick hisse'f war thar ef ye'd
    a hearn him shout.

An' then the sisters, they broke in an' shook thar
    petticoats
An' frum that on thar singin' warnt accordin'
    ter thar notes.
Ol' Grimes, he rubbed his cheek an' neck an'
    sot up sech a cry;
An' all at onct, the Pa'son put his han' up ter
    his eye.

An' then he struck out lef' an' right, an' pawed about the a'r
Ez ef he hed the tremens, an' the snakes' they hed him thar.
He jumped about three feet, an' then went under out o' sight,
An' when the good man made the bank, ye orter'v seen him kite.

Some went this way an' some went that, an' some rolled on the groun',
An' in two shakes o' a sheep's tail, thar warn't a soul aroun',
They hed stirred up a hornet's nes' thar in that little knoll,
An' that's what caused ev'ry one ter lose thar se'f-control.

It war a Presbyterian trick, at leas' I'm satisfied
They planted that air ho'net's nes' down by the water's side,
Fur ever sence the neighborhood, with sprinklin' hez been cu'sed,
While not a single critter thar hez ever been immu'sed.

Thar's nothin' parfec' in this worl', ez my ph'l-
   osophy,
But why the Lo'd permitted this, is a mystery
   ter me,
Fur every member struck fur hum, an' lef' us in
   the lu'ch,
An' so that pesky ho'net's nes' broke up our
   Baptist chu'ch.

TO MY BOOKS.

'Tis not around the festive board,
   Where brilliant revelry attends,
To pledge in superficial word
   And bated breath, I meet my friends;
A tiny room above the stair,
   Which out upon the city looks;
I nightly come and greet them there,
   My noble, trusty friends—my books.

Iv'e plodded on my weary way;
   Known fortune's smiles and fortune's frowns.
Groped in darkness, basked in day;
   In brief, I've had my ups and downs.
Yet with a purpose fixed as fate,
   You pointed to the higher goal,
Whence strive the gifted and the great,
   The noble and the pure of soul.

TO MY BOOKS.

You lured me first to virtue's side
  By visions of the pure ideal,
And taught me by a wisdom wide,
  That the unseen is the real.
Whatever be our woe or weal,
  Our aspirations or our fears,
On all material things the seal
  Of death is set—and vain our tears.

We've soared together starry heights,
  Explored the mysteries of space;
Traced, through many sleepless nights,
  The singing spheres in endless chase.
We've peeped into the opaque earth;
  Gone out upon the trackless sea;
Strolled through brilliant halls of mirth,
  And wept midst scenes of misery.

Through realms were reign the kings of thought,
  You've led me with a loving hand—
Where learning's priceless gems are sought
  And science waves her magic wand.

How apt a scholar I have been—
    If love and service be the gauging—
For all may not the laurel win
    The honors in the war we're waging.

But time is fleeting, I have known
    Full half the span the prophet told;
And, comrades, I am free to own,
    For it is true, "I'm growing old."
Some night the lamp will not be lit,
    And vacant be the easy chair,
And he who used to bide in it,
    Be gone, ah! who can answer where?

KNOX'S LANDING, MISSISSIPPI.

Knox's is what they call it, an' hev fur this forty
    years,
An' alus will, I reckon, leastwise, sir, the name
    appears
Ter stick ter this hyar landin' like the bark
    aroun' a tree—
An' ef its Knox ye air lookin' fur, howdy? fur
    that's me.

Goin' down the river, eh, on the boat ter New
    Orleans?
Moughty pleasant trip ter take, fine climate an'
    splen'd scenes.
I've made it many a time, in pioneer days, ye
    know,
Afore they thought o' railroads, an' when boats
    war made ter go.

But lookin' arter the farm hez kept me at hum
    o' late,
Then ye know that keers with age air apt ter
    accumulate,
An' seven thousan' acres ain't no truck patch,
    ye'll allow,
When labor's ez unsartin ez its gittin' ter be now.

So ye'r' an editor, an' want ter write 'bout
    we-uns hyar,
An' put us in the paper? Waal, I'd rether ye
    would'nt, sir—
But ef ye mus' hev readin, why then, lemme see
    —oh, waal,
Mebbe I mought gin ye suthin' 'bout good enough
    ter tell.

Suthin' like them air novils ez ye city fellers
    writes,
'Bout shipwrecks an' adventures an' all them
    sort o' sights,
Fus' rate ter pass the time on, when ye've nothin'
    else, mebbe,
So then git out yer pencil, ye shell hev it; lemme
    see.

We fus' kem hyar in forty an' it happened jes
    this way,
An' a lunlier spot ye would'nt fin' in all America.
We war jes like that air fus' pa'r in thar prime-
    val hum,
Without the fruit an' shrubbery, but all them
    things hev kem.

Waal, ye've heard about the bustin' o' the
    Washington? Eh, O,
Ye haint? I don't wonder, fur it war a long
    time ago.
I war pilot on that boat when she let her kittles
    fly,
An' I'll not furgit it, straunger, ontil the day I
    die.

Jes how many thar war los' the accounts all
    disagree,
But I know I reached the shor', an' another one
    with me,
An' as ter who it war, ye'll learn afore my story's
    through,
An' don't think that I'm romancin', fur ev'ry
    word is true.

Waal, the fus thing that I knowed, I war
    floatin' in the stream,
When I notic'd jes ahead, suthin' in the fire-
    light gleam—
Fur the wreck war all ablaze—an' it drifted
    silently,
Like a bunch o' airy foam, keepin' company
    with me.

An' I dunno why it war, but somehow I felt
    empelled
Ter swim in that derection, an' I reached it an'
    then yelled,
Fur jes then a suddent blaze lighted up the
    lunly place,
An' I saw it war a female starin' me in the face.

She never riz a whimper, an' war woman-like,
    resigned,
But I didn't hev the heart fur ter leave her thar
    behin',
An' I said, I'm gwine ter take this hyar helpless
    one ashor'
Or thar's two o' us shell drown; an' look thar,
    outside the door—

That's her thar in the garden—she's a little ol'er now,
Not much ter be writin' 'bout at sixty, ye'll allow—
Thar's the bell, the boat's ready ter continer on her trip,
An' ef ye print my story, call it Knox o' Mississip.

WHAT THE CLOCK SAID.

" Tick! Tick! Tick! Tick! "
Always the same monotonous click—
Toiling on in the old fashioned way,
With never a moment for rest or play,
And with never a word but this to say:
      " Tick! Tick! Tick! Tick! "

"Tick! Tick! Tick! Tick!"
Oh, pause, for my heart is sore and sick!
I'm nearing the end of life's brief race,
And why will you chase, and chase, and chase?
The answer came from the crystal face:
      " Tick! Tick! Tick! Tick! "

" Tick! Tick! Tick! Tick! "
Stop, I say! 'Tis a scurrilous trick!
Hast thou no feeling nor sympathy
For mortal man in his misery?
Stay, unfold the great mystery!
      " Tick! Tick! Tick! Tick?! "

"Tick! Tick! Tick! Tick!"
Oh, then, 'tis onward you lead us, quick—
Teach us to look to the other side
Of the river they call so dark and wide.
I paused, and thus the clock replied:
    "Tick! Tick! Tick! Tick!"

"Tick! Tick! Tick! Tick!"
The night is gathering 'round me thick!
Oh, say, shall I see the outer day?
Shall the soul live that has learned to pray?
The old clock has but this to say:
    "Tick! Tick! Tick! Tick!"

ZEKE SLABSIDES.

Tim Juggles was a butcher's son, of Southern Illinois,
Who spent his early youth in winning pins from other boys,
Till the fuz 'pon his upper lip began to venture out,
When he went into the bus'ness of a steamboat roustabout.
He took his reg'lar rations in, of hard-tack, hash and junk,
And stole promiscuously his naps from sack pile, plank and bunk.
Till finally he found his wealth in currency did range
Near sixteen dollars and six bits, all in good silver change.

Tim sat a moment on the deck, still gazing on
    his tin,
Then grasp'd a pen, and wrote and sent his
    resignation in:
And from a busted gambler he purchased dice
    and truck,
And opened right upon the spot a bank of
    chuckaluck.
For months he prospered handsomely in raking
    in the cash,
When to his finances there came one day an
    awful smash;
And just to show that wealth has wings, and
    very often flies,
I'll give the circumstance in full, which hap-
    pened in this wise:

Zeke Slabsides was dishwasher upon that same
    steamboat—
Of bell-crown'ed fashion was his hat, and coun-
    try jeans his coat,
But the way he made the suds fly, caus'd all to
    stop and look,
And vow that he was business in what he under-
    took.

One day, when the cook's eye was turned away
    from Zekiel's tub,
He sold to a deck passenger a quarter's worth of
    grub,
And straightway started for the stern, till just
    abaft the crank,
He squatted down upon the deck, and went for
    Juggles' bank.

Zeke slapped his quarter on the ace, and rushed
    the gambling through
Upon a scale that soon made Tim shell out his
    bottom sou;
And when the cook went back to see what Zekiel
    could be at,
He found him with all Juggles' wealth stowed in
    his bell-crowned hat.
When Juggles saw his bank was broke, ses he,
    "There's something wrong,"
And straightway curs'd a stream of oaths, un-
    usually long.
He swore that he could lick the Jake that play'd
    that thing on him;
And, reaching forth for Zekiel, took him in the
    jaw, *ca-bim!*

Zeke set his hat upon a box, and on Tim set his eye,
And said, "ef ye hev any friends, jest bid them now good-bye,"
And, striking from his shoulder, give him such a lively clout:
That Juggles found to his surprise that he was knocked clear out.
The moral of this story is, as plainly can be seen,
That if all is not gold that shines, some ripe fruit may look green.
And those who spend their energies in prating of ill-luck,
May see how easy fortune yields, when once attacked with pluck.

CAUGHT UNAWARES.

Why, Dora, love, this look of secrecy?
   Shedding thy furtive glances here and there;
   Say, has obtrusion caught thee unaware?
Oh, pet, I see all is not well with thee.

Doth doubt my love, I'll seal it with a kiss,
   And warrant not to disarrange thy bangs.
   What's the reason she still fire hangs?
I ne'er before knew her so coy as this.

Nay, tell me all, doth the long-buried years
   Hold in their calm embrace, an earlier flame?
   And was thou fondly gazing on the same
In photograph? If nay, oh, whence these fears?

Why push the sofa closer to the wall
   And motion with thine eyes towards the door?
   I never saw you act this way before;
Oh, Dora, dear, have you no word at all?

Keep me not in suspense; what is it, sweet,
  That puts you at this time so off your feed?
Whence these myster'us bundles, what's the need
Covering everything up so complete? [need

"Hist! hist!" she said, as twitching at my sleeve,
  "Keep quiet, or you'll give us clean away;
I have been hiding things the livelong day;
Dearest, do you forget 'tis Christmas eve?"

PICKET'S POSTOFFICE, TENNESSEE.

Picket's? waal, this is it,
   But the orfice is whar
Ye see that smoke risin'
   Frum the shed over thar,
   Leas' sence the row war hyar.

Ef men can't git along
   Without thar reg'lar fight,
Why don't they fust a'journ
   Ter a convenient site
   Afore they vent thar spite?

Leastwise, at honest folks,
   Who's morally inclined,
An hold different views
   On matters o' this kind,
   An don't drink till thar blind

Ez them-uns did that night,
   When they bu'nt down the stor'—
Thar war twenty o' em,
   An some say thar war mo'
   Hitched thar nags 'roun' the do'.

Some went ter pitchin quoits,
    An' some sot on a rail,
An' drunk thar straight "moonshine"
    Frum the distil'ry pail
    An' waited fur the mail.

Now, ev'rything went smooth
    Till I fouched in the bags,
Then the boys kem an' sot
    Aroun' on the nail kegs,
    Full 'n lim'er, ter, ez rags.

An' jawed an' growled an' cussed
    Ontil I said thar's two
Letters this time, all tol',
    An' Reno, thar fur ye—
    An' he tuk em frum me.

Then Bowles, he made a speech,
    An' went on ter declar'
That ev'rything fur one
    An' none for none else thar
    Warn't 'zactly on the squar'.

An' ez fur the orfice,
　　Why h—ll wur full o' sech;
An' so it war o' mails
　　Like them air Yankees fetch—
　　Bad senterments ter tech.

Fur, 'fore ye could say it,
　　A keg upsot the lamp!
An' the place war afire—
　　I felt 'twar time ter tramp—
　　Didn't save a postage stamp.

An' this is all 'ats lef',
　　An' it grieves me ter see
N'thin but a heap o' rocks
　　Whar the orfice ust t'r be—
　　No more P. M. fur me.

THE MYSTERIOUS SUICIDE.

'Twas evening in St. Louis, and the streets were
    all aglow
With the votaries of fashion that were strolling
    to and fro,
Sleek men and stylish women passed in pano-
    ramic view,
With an ease that indicated they'd nothing else
    to do.

But among them loitered one, who seemed in-
    different
To everything about him, as his nervous steps
    he bent.
His right hand grasped a grip-sack, while all his
    clothing showed,
By their travel-stained appearance, he'd been
    long upon the road.

Not an eye of recognition beamed 'pon him
    from the throng,
But keeping pace he murmured, in a monotone,
    a song,
A maudlin repetition, and the words he spoke
    were these:
"We are bound for an island in the far off
    Southern seas."

Thus he hummed till the twilight settled down
    and all dispersed,
And then he fell to weeping, till I thought his
    heart would burst.
"Oh!" he cried, "they have left me here to
    bear it all alone,"
And, overcome with anguish, he sat down upon
    a stone.

His pallid brow was furrowed deep with many
    lines of care,
And round about it clustered tufts of premature
    gray hair;
While his thin and haggard features and un-
    kempt locks combined
To convince me some great sorrow was preying
    on his mind.

And I said, "What's the matter, mister, tell me, I implore,
Have your mines in Colorado failed to pan out paying ore?
Dost pine for lack of capital to put down another hole —
Or have you been familiar with the rosy flowing bowl?

"Perhaps it was on 'futures' that you staked your little pile,
And the result retired you from the market for awhile;
Or it may be you're in mourning for some departed trust
That fed your mind on lux'ry and your stomach on a crust."

"Friend, you're wrong," he said; "it isn't dissipation that ails me,
Nor have financial failures brought about the wreck you see;
On the other hand I flourish on the summit of the boom,
'Til this ceaseless clamor struck me, and I fled in search of room.

"I have left home and kindred—traveled far
    and traveled wide,
But I hear it still ringing in my ears on every
    side;
All the earth is impregnated, and the very winds
    are schooled
To go howling in my ears: Jay Gould, Jay
    Gould, Jay G-o-uld!"

Here he rose, and, pressing forward, quickly
    sought the towering crest
Of the famous iron structure, saying, "Surely,
    here is rest;
For the tired heart o'erburdened 'tis a blessed
    privilege—"
"Yer's your extra! latest news, Jay Gould has
    bought the bridge!"

"Well, I'm blowed," he said, and straightway
    laid his coat and hat aside—
Took a last look at the city, scanned the country
    far and wide;
Climbed o'er the outer railing, gave one tremen-
    dous skip,
Turned a somersault and lit in the turbid
    Mississip'.

HE WANTED TO BE COUNTED IN.

Thar war a feller named Si Blivin 'at follered
    flat-boatin' on the Mississip',
He war the durndes' critter fur makin a noise,
    and war alus holerin' "let 'er rip!"
Thar war nuthin' ye could git up but this galoot
    'ou'd be browsin' 'roun', and dog my skin,
Ef ye'd start a game o' keard er any other kin'
    o' amusement, he war dead sure fer ter
    want ter be counted in.

But when the boat got in a clus' plac' an' pullin'
    war ter be done, then 'n th'r
He'd rassle with a sweep till the ol' skow'd
    shake like a steam engine hed holt o' her,
An' ter see him lay fur an oar looked like deer
    goin' ter bounce a stake 'n rail fence,
And he snap 'em in two in a business-like way,
    jes ez though he didn't keer a continental
    'bout the expense.

But the purties' thing war ter watch him hist a
    jug an' drink out o' it with one han',
Wun o' them accomplishments that mus' be seed
    'fore ye kin fully understan'.
An' ye could hear the liquor a sloshin' down his
    inerds jes edzacly ez though
He war holler plum ter his feet an' thar was
    plenty o' room ter stow it 'way down thar
    below.

Whenever the ol' "broadho'n" hed ter kem ter
    fur wind' er anything o' that kin',
Si'd shoulder his gun 'n strike for the swamp,
    with his yeller dog follerin' behin',
An' they waltz aroun' in the cottonwood ontil
    they struck a fat buc' er a bar,
When he'd blaze 'way and fur the next week er
    two thar' be game fur the boat's crew
    an' ter spar'.

Ye never seed sech a critter ter git his work in,
    jes ez ef it war boy's play,
Fur he war one o' them narterel bo'n genuses
    that everything seems ter run thar way.

A philosopher plum' through an' looked on everything ez a plain matter o' fac',
An he'd snatch a hen roost bal'headed whenever he felt that it war chickens that the crew o' the boat mos' lacked.

One day they kem ter at Napole'n jes ter take a little res' an' see the sights,
Fur it war a lively place, full o' saloons 'n all kin' o' games 'n free fights.
Si tried his han' at mos' everything, but didn't hol' his reg'lar luc' an' couldn't win,
So he goes cavortin' roun' till he struck a row an' said ef they hed no objections he like ter be counted in.

An' he shed his duster an' in he sailed for an hour, or mebbe it war mor',
An' all the time he war busier 'n he'd been fur several season afor'.
When, at las' the smoke hed cleared away, the pieces war picked up an' stowed in a pile,
But they couldn't find enough o' any one critter so 's ter put him tergether in any sort o' style.

Si seein' how things war with nothin' ter draw
    ter but one leg, said with a sickly grin;
"Waal, now, ef this hyar's a funeral that ye air
    a fixin' fur ye kin jes count me in."
An' they planted him down thar in Arkansas
    under the cottonwoods an' mosses,
An' straunger, when ye kem ter talk 'bout yer
    good men, don't furgit ol' Si Blivin. fur I
    tell ye he war one o' the hosses.

THE MEMBER FROM COHOES.

'Twar in the Capitol
  That this epersode occurred,
An' that I tuk a han' myself,
  It mus'nt be inferred,
  I state jes what I've heard,

The legislators all 'd met,
  Each member hed his cha'r,
When Colonel Brooks o' Choctaw said:
  "Who's that over thar?
  Is this hyar on the squar'?"

He p'nted ter a person,
  With glasses on his nose,
Who answered: "I's de mem'er
  Frum de Par'h o' Cohoes,
  Who else 'ould ye suppose."

Then Gen'ral Parsons riz 'n said:
  "I 'low ez that ain't so,
That darky setting in that cha'r 's
    My ol' barber Jo —
    The Yankees freed, ye know."

Ef a pin 'd been inserted
  In each white member's seat,
He couldn't any quicker
    Hev risen ter his feet,
    The upris'n war complete.

The little scene that follered,
  I'm sorry ter relate,
Did not reflec' credit
    On the helmsmen o' a state,
    Assembled fur debate.

When order war resumed
  It war plain thar war in store
A number of repairs,
    But that member never more
    Warmed a seat 'pon that floor.

THE MYSTIFIED TRAVELLER.

A gamin rushing through the street,
　The latest news proclaimed,
And to the people that he'd meet
　This startling caption named:
"All about the coffer-dam,
　With full accounts to date
Of the great feat of Uncle Sam—
　Blowin' up Hell-Gate!"

To whom a countryman replied:
　"I'll buy your latest news.
Now can you help me to decide
　Which of these streets to choose,
Which takes me to the river pier?—
　I fear I'm somewhat late."
"Keep right ahead—papers yer?
　All about Hell-Gate."

"Manhattan's isle is densely packed,
    Manhattan's isle is small,
And yet creation has been sacked
    To fill her houses tall.
Whence comes this crowd of dubious worth,
    As though to tempt their fate?
Has Castle-Garden belched them forth?"
" 'Splosion at Hell Gate."

"Your summer sun beats fierce and hot;
    Some cooler clime I'd seek,
Where pyramids of brick are not,
    And board is less per week.
Which passage would you recommend?—
    For I must emigrate."
"Crowds from the city daily wend,—
    Big travel through Hell-Gate."

"One question more I'd ask, young man—
    Which way sail they, I pray?
Steam they beneath the bridge's span,
    Or down the open bay?
Fair winds have blown in golden fruit
    From many a tropic state—
Where spy we first the shallop's shoot?"
    "All about Hell-Gate."

THE MYSTIFIED TRAVELLER.

"Indeed? why, then, I must decline,"
  The traveller replied,
And striking out in a bee line,
  To Jersey City hied;
And when his stalwart form that night
  A Pullman sleeper pressed,
He sighed—"Hell-Gate not for me, quite;
  I'd rather chance the West."

LINGUISTIC LORE.

Erastus Fitzhugh was his name,
A society man of local fame.

Parted his hair in the middle, wore
Mutton chop whiskers, age thirty-four.

He attended parties, dinners, balls,
Operas, plays and lecture halls.

Again, for variety, would spend
An evening with some lady friend.

But his better hold was the charming way
He got in his work on New Year's Day.

And candor compels me here to state
He started early and went it late.

And, viewing the viands, he would say,
"Ah! madam, this is ah! *recherche.*"

So from house to house Mr. Fitzhugh went,
And paid to each the same compliment.

Till a hundred matrons, one and all,
Boasted of Mr. Fitzhugh's call,

And said, in a kind of taunting way,
That he called her table *recherche*,

And the happy creatures still adore
Mr. Fitzhugh, of linguistic lore,

Never suspecting the French displayed
Was his only foreign stock in trade.

FIT WITH GRANT.

Have you seen the Gin'rel? Waal, he's now in
   town,
  Come out from Washington on a little chase.
We met jes' now ez I wuz a comin' down
   The street, the fus time sence the war, face
     to face,
But it 'peard ez ef he did'nt remember me,
Though I fit with him in eighteen sixty-three.

I understan' they've 'pinted a committee
  To show him aroun' an' hev a bankit spread,
An' tender him the freedom o' the city
  In recognition o' the part that he played
In savin' this hyar great lan' o' liberty—
When we wuz fitin' it out in sixty-three.

An' yit, I've no pension ner quarter section,
   Ner any interes' in Uncle Sam's farms.
You see, him an' me severed our connection,
   An' swung apart afore Lee laid down his arms,
Which seems mighty curious, I mus' agree,
Fur a man who'd fit with Grant in sixty-three.

I've often seen the Gin'rel during battle—
   Fur he was ginerally at the front, 'bout then,
An' seemed to rether like the roar an' rattle—
   An' I low he looks 'bout the same now ez when
I fit with him away back in sixty-three—
Doin' my level bes' fur Gin'rel Lee!

ATONEMENT.

A worthy woman, sick and poor,
Begged her bread from door to door.

One said: "We'd nothing left to-day."
The woman bowed, and walked away.

Another—"We have guests within;
Move on and don't be bothering."

Entering an adjoining gate,
She climbed the steps and stood and wait.

But when the servant came, she said:
"Every one has gone to bed."

Thus fruitlessly the woman sought
For food, for no one gave her aught.

And, overcome with woe, she bowed
Her weary head and wept aloud,

And cried, "They will not—can not—feel
That never wanted for a meal!"

ATONEMENT.

But, turning to retrace her way,
She saw a house, where brilliantly

The lights were burning, and the air
Was musical with voices there.

"Oh! surely they will not deny
Me help!" she said, and presently

Sought the door, and rung the bell.
The mistress came, and said: "Pray, tell

Me what it is that I can do
At this late hour, madam, for you?"

The simple story was retold.
The mistress answered, "Here is gold,

Go purchase for your children bread."
The woman turned and quickly fled,

Forgetting all she had endured
In the blessing thus secured.

MORAL.

Though many heeded not her call,
The one who gave atoned for all.

THE TRUE CREED.

A toiler wrought
Till his thrift brought
Wealth and position, when he sought
The polite quarter of the town,
And in good fashion settled down.

An idler passed,
And said: "I fast,
And roam the streets a poor outcast,
In a land of plenty. But there
Is a place 'll know no millionaire."

In time they died,
And straightway hied
The man who wrought to Peter's side,
Who said: "Pass to thy higher state;"
But the idler never reached the gate.

WATERING THE STOCKS.

Jones said the hall was splendid—nothing like it in the land—
And only lacked a fountain to make it really grand;
    In the center it should stand.

Then Watts drew up a paper, and remarked, "We'll have that, too,
And raise it by subscription;" when the Deacon said, " Don't you,
    I will put the whole thing through."

That's how the Mississippi came to flow abundantly
Through the commercial temple; but it never did agree
    With the 'Change fraternity.

While the scene that came about on the dedica-
 tion day
Should never be repeated by those gentlemen
 if they
  Wouldn't give themselves away.

'Twas shocking how the Major took a sup, then
 wheeled about
And made a hasty exit; telling those along the
 route,
  "Boys, I pass, that lifts me out."

Next came a German brother, who exclaimed,
 "Das ist nicht bier.
Donner und blitzen! ich bin seek!" and he, too,
 did disappear
  With some others in his rear.

And they followed till the room was as bare as
 it could be,
When the President arose, and addressed himself to me:
  "Why is this stampede?" said he.

I pointed to the fountain, and replied: "The
 trouble's there;
You have watered all their stocks, and there's
 music in the air—
 All is panic everywhere.

That's all I know about it, and I hope you will
 refrain
Hereafter from alluding to the circumstance
 again,
 Yours truly, I remain.

THE MARTYR.

A shadow of her former self,
    She plied her household cares,
And daily scoured each cupboard shelf,
    And polished up the wares,
And diligently gave her thoughts
    To these minute affairs.

She took no note of social life,
    Which many love to court,
A higher aim, a nobler strife,
    Had come to be her forte,
And patiently she toiled and strove
    To gain a good report.

No more she sought her husband's smile,
    The children ceased to cheer,
The parlor could no more beguile,
    Her place was in the rear.
Where her fixed purpose she pursued
    No matter who was near.

Each evening saw her thinner grow,
    The lines more tightly drawn
About her face; the former glow
    Of her bright eyes was gone.
When, lo! there came a sudden cry,
    And her life's work was done.

They found her stretched upon the floor,
    A masher in her hand,
A cockroach she had failed to gore
    Smiled from a crevice, and
A handsome young wife reigns supreme
    Where once she did command.

THE WABASH RANGER.

A demon they called him—that wuz the word,
    He hed no feelin' fur man or woman,
An' the Sheriff agreed he'd never heard
    O' a critter that wuz so inhuman.

Why, he tho't nothin' of dousin' a glim
    An' sett'n a widder ter wearin' sable.
Ez fur orphans, 't warn't worryin him
    Ef they foun' no vituals on the table.

He'd pull out his navy an' bang away,
    An' bore a hole through a healthy granger,
Then express regrets that he couldn't stay
    Ter the funeral, this Wabash Ranger.

But one mornin' the prison henges swung
    An' a lady enter'd whos' grace 'n beauty
War whisper'd 'roun' on ev'ry tongue,
    An' all bowed thar heads ez 't wuz their duty.

An' she raised her eyes till they caught the gaze
    O' the outlaw who his cell wuz pacin',
When he suduntly stop'ed his nervous ways,
    An the two stood still each other facin'.

Then she laid her hand on the iron door,
    'Twuz white as snow an' a diamon glistened,
An a look that he mo'ght hev seen afor'
    Beamed frum her eyes ez he stood an' listened.

"Here is a bunch of flowers and there are clothes,
    Go cleanse your body and heal your gashes,
And here is a Bible, God only knows,"—
    An' the tears fell fas' frum her silken lashes.

Then the outer hinges swung wide an' quick,
    Closed behind the mysterious straunger,
An' ever sence that day a chil' could lick
    The game an' trucculent Wabash Ranger.

TOBE GRAY.

  Es ter Tobe Gray,
  He worked hyar way
  Back at a time—
  A-settin rhyme
  An' prose an' ads,
When mos' o' you uns hyar war tads.

  Ol' Tobe warn't much
  On clothes an' sech,
  An' ust ter say:
  I'll spen' my pay
  Inside my vest—
Things ez tastes good suits me the best."

  He'd nuss hez type
  When fat war ripe,
  Then take a walk
  Er set an' talk
  At the caboose
'Till ye'd think the ol' man's tongue war loose.

'Bout everythin'
Wo'th mentionin',
He'd talk about,
Day in an' out,
An' keep hez eye
On the " growler " when it war nigh.

But one day he
Remarked ter me,
"I'm all afire
Inside me hyar,"
An' gin ter shout
"I'm pestered with the stumache drought."

We got him beer
An' tried ter cheer
His sperits up—
He took a sup
An' then he cried
"It's my last *take*, I 'low," an' died.

He warn't perfec'—
Ye kent expec'
A man ter be
That way ye see,
More'n a woman—
We loved him 'cause he war so human.

DRAW ONE.*

He rode into town from the Brazos, and
    Meekly called for his supper and bed—
A dark-eyed gent with a nervous hand
    And a belt overflush with cold lead.

His speech had the usual front-tier flow—
    As he said to the waiter man near,
"Bring me some fried flitch and eggs and co-
    F-fee,"—he stuttered perceptibly here.

But there was eloquence in his eyes,
    And so the waiter man he caught on,
And to the cook repeated the size
    Of the order, and ended, "Draw One!"

But scarce had the echoes died away,
    When something tore past him whir-rr-iz,
And though he doesn't claim it, I'm free to say,
    The best time out of Austin is his.

And now when a gent with wild flowing hair
    Comes up from the land of the sun,
"Coffee" is the word they're using where
    They formerly called out "Draw One!"

*A Cup of Coffee.

THE MATE OF THE MARIA.

Ez ter that yarn 'bout Knox, the mate,
Fact is, boys, that I kin' o' hate
Ter stir up by-gones! 'Tain't no use
Turnin' them air ol' times loose,
Better let em res', fur durn my eyes,
Ef ye shake the pas' the gos's 'll rise.

But ef I mus', why then hyar goes,
"Bad Knox" they called 'm, an' I 'spose
He war rough! Why, he'd ruther fight
'Un eat his supper any night;
An ef ye want'd ter make him sick,
Jes name some critter he couldn't lick.

He'd lam a roust'r fur exercise,
An' put down a riot 'fore 't could rise,
Ef he had ter whale the whol' deck crew,
An' bust up a game of chuc'luck, too,
Then waltz back aft an' yell "freight pile,"
When thar warn't a landin' in ten mile.

He war a stun'r, sure's yer bo'n,
An' ye jes orter hev seed the ho'n
He could hol'—four fingers er mo'
Of "Robinson County." Ye mought po'r
Licker in 'm till ye'd bus' the bar,
An' still he'd kem up smilin' thar.

That war Knox! Waal, one stormy night
Jes ez Red River hev en sight,
We sot 'roun the stove near the stun
Watchin' the pitchy pine knots bu'n,
Till one by one we drapped ter sleep
Promiscusly ez a flock o' sheep.

When on a sud'ent thar kem a crash,
An then we felt the hot steam flash,
People war scatter'd hyar an' thar—
In the river an' everywhar,
She'd bus' her bilers an' war on fire,
An' that war the end of the ol' Mariar.

But whar war Knox? D' ye think he swum
Ter the sho' an lef' the res' ter kem?
Not much, ye bet, that warn't his style,
Ye could hear his voice 'bout ten mile—
Hear that wicked ol' sinner shout,
"Stan' by an' help these wimmen out."

He pulled em from the bu'nin' wreck,
An' tossen' 'em on the for'ard deck,
Tol' 'em ter make fur the neardes' sho'
While he went back ter s'arch fur mo'.
Ye never seed a sight ter compar'
With the way Knox got his work in thar.

But soon the fire begun ter bite
The water's edge, an' then the light
Went out, an' darkness set'led in,
But Knox kep' yel'in like all sin:
"Ef the darned galoots'd done 'z I said
I'd hev saved 'em all!" Bad Knox war dead.

Now, I don't kno' whar his sperit went,
Fur he war ter durn busy ter repent,
But I 'low ef ye could git the vote
O' them he saved frum the bu'nin' boat,
The verdic' 'uld be—bes' thing ter do,
Fur ol' Saint Peter ter pass him through.

TO A SOLDIER OF THE UNION.

'Twas not ambition, nor the tinsel show
Of conquest to dispoil a weaker foe
Nerved you to leave your hallowed home and go,
Oh, warrior of our later, broader day,
And bear our flag victorious in the fray.

Nor yet for fame, the old, old theme and cry,
That leads the noblest to dare and die,
But love for man and for humanity
And the oppressed. We know that thou didst feel
The blow that smote the slave—the tyrant's heel.

'Tis meet the laurel 'round the brow should cling,
Whose only boast is that of suffering;
Who claims no battles won—no conquering—
Taking the vanquished brother to thy breast,
And trusting to the future all the rest.

So shall thy deeds live on through coming years
In spectral majesty—when disappears
Thy bent and aged form, and dried the tears
Which from affection's fountains still must flow,
Till all who knew and loved thee are laid low.

THE CHECOT ELECTION.

Thar's nothin' really certain in this sinful worl' o' ours,
An' a Christian may git euchred with a hand o' trumps an' bowers.
An' there's times when moral suason ceases to perform its part,
An' we air fo'ced to take a hand in the military art.

To make more clear, a circumstance which I will jes explain,
Occurred at Checot City at the close of a campaign.
Our candidate fur Governor wuz Judge Albert Sidney Brent,
While the radicals were boomin' that yeller Jones, o' Kent.

We knew that the majority war likely with the mob,
An' thought it statesmanlike that we put up a little job.
"Fur truth an' jestice must prevail," said honest Pa'son Tripp,
"Ef we heve ter ferry voters frum 'cross the Mississip'."

The pollin' went on quietly ter closin' time, an we
Felt certain we hed scooped 'em by a big majority.
"To the casual observer," said the Jedge, "all is fixed,"
But we subsequently learned that affairs war kind o' mixed.

Fur when the vote war counted, Rice, that Yankee Jedge, announced
"'That all the ex-confed'rates hed been beautifully bounced."
When Gineral Wirt, o' Natchez, immediately arose,
An' vowed 'twar our allies hed Jones' money in thar clothes.

Then the Jedge looked much surprised an' he
    raised the cry o' fraud:
Said the principles o' jestice war 'bout ter be
    outlawed.
An' leapin' on a whiskey bar'l orated ter the
    crowd,
How they'd been wrongly influ'nced in thar
    votin' he allowed.

When ter the great surprise o' all, that barrel head
    went in,
An' I grieve I hev ter say it, the Jedge settled
    ter his chin,
When Sandy Smith, o' Rodney, gev the thing a
    healthy kick,
An' 'way it went a rollin' with the Jedge towards
    the crick.

Hank Johnston yelled, "look out below," Jack
    Sanders, "let her rip,"
When I tu'ned an' saw both sides fur a fight
    begin ter strip.
A pistol ball come whizzin' by an' cut away the
    skin
O' this hyar car; ye see its gone—when every
    man waltzed in.

Frum a second story winder Jones observed he
"presumed"—
When a boulder called upon him an' his remarks
war doomed,
An another colored statesman who said "I an-
tic'pate"—
An' broad "eyther" used fur "either" met with a
similar fate.

'Twar shockin' fur ter listen ter the navy pistols
bark,
An' I jedge that mighty few o' em ever missed
thar mark.
Fur when the sun went down upon the animated
scene,
Some twenty-three dead Africans war stretched
out on the green.

We corded up the corpses jes like ranks o'
cottonwood,
An' the Coroner went through 'em in lots the
best he could.
Told the jury 'twar a cl'ar case, jes trot the
thing along,
An' they returned a verdict, "met thar death
from vutin' wrong."

Thar's nothin' really certain in this sinful worl'
    o' ours,
An' a Christian may git euchred with a han' o'
    trumps an' bowers;
When our noblest institutions air successfully
    assailed,
An' a man is never happy until arter he's been
    whaled.

THE PAUPER.

Aged and poor, and broken down,
And scarcely noticed by the town,
    For home and friends he'd none,
A relic of departed years,
This the sound that greets his ears—
    "I say, old man, move on!"

Sometimes he asked for charity,
But 'las for human sympathy!
    For dumb was every one,
Save the voice which repeated o'er
The language uttered just before,
    "I say, old man, move on!"

But in good time, kind nature brought
Surcease of sorrow, and they sought
    To solve the mystery,
"Died of want," the jury returned,
"General Brown," his name they learned,
    Confed'rate Cavalry.

DEACON BARKER'S PHILOSOPHY.

I hol' the worl' ain't goin' back,
Ez some fo'ks say; taint a fact,
It's goin' for'ard right along
With all its sinfulness an' wrong;
An' ef the good Lo'd now an' then
Draws in the lines, le's say, Amen,

An' stop our headlong pace, an' wait
Till we kin see our way mo' straight.
An' spen' some time a givin' thanks
Fur what we hev, an' not like cranks
Go fin'in fault with God 'n man
'Thout lendin' either one a han'.

'Taint the hones' thing ter do,
Er treatin' Him ez He treats you,
Who sen's the changin' seasons 'roun'
To bless the country an' the town,
'An marks the little sparrer's fall,
An' loves His chil'ren one an' all.

Thar's mo' o' sunshine than o' cloud
In this ol' world, I've alus 'lowed,
But when we leave the narrer track,
Thar's alus trouble gittin' back,
An' takes a little sufferin'
For' we git started on agin'.

THE RAID OF THE HOPPER.

'Twas just beyond the Kansas line, or somewhere thereabout,
A veteran hopper squole a squeal, then shrieked an awful shout,
Calling all his tribe to arms, from the Rocky Mountain peaks
To the sacred reservations, set apart for Sioux and Creeks.

There was marshalling in the valley, there was darkness in the air,
And soon about ten hundred billion fresh recruits were there,
Old Xerxes with his legions could not have taken a trick,
For they were piled upon the ground full twenty-three miles thick.

THE RAID OF THE HOPPER. 147

Well, one morning bright and early, as Sol began to throw
His regenerating glances on the broad expanse below,
The commander looked about him from the limb of a huge oak,
And to his lusty followers, his little piece he spoke:

"Brave comrades, there lies Kansas, rich in esculents and grains,
And beyond far-famed Missouri stretches out her fertile plains,
We'll go through it like a whirlwind, so forward, follow me!"
You'd've thought the way they skipped, that each hopper was a flea.

And they raided like true bummers — laid fields and gardens waste—
Never left behind a nibble, for either man or beast,
Of anything to subsist on—who seeing their sad fate,
Concluded they had better get right up and emigrate.

Some struck the river and come south, and some
　　went overland,
And people seeing them hard up, reached out a
　　helping hand,
Until the conquering hopper held undisputed
　　sway
Of all the territory that thereabouts did lay.

This is how the matter rested on closing the
　　campaign;
But early in the coming spring, the hoppers
　　hopped again.
Then they crossed into Missouri, which made
　　our Governor rave,
And vow that Providence alone our noble State
　　could save.

And straight he set apart a day for fasting and
　　for prayer,
Requesting every citizen "to try his hand some-
　　where,
For the race ain't always to the swift, nor the
　　battle to the strong,
And a little good old-fashioned grace might help
　　the thing along."

But some speculating Yankee, of an inquiring mind,
Began to make experiments on the dead he found behind,
He was an entomologist of eminent degree,
And very soon obtained results surprising for to see.

He scooped a peck of hoppers, and to a baker hied,
Had some made into pudding, some in dumpling, and some fried;
Then he spread a splendid banquet, of dishes he'd prepared,
Which a number of professors and men of learning shared.

One passed upon a second joint, and another on a wing,
And sending up their plates again, pronounced it just the thing;
And before the meal was over, each guest had made a boast
That he much preferred fried hopper to snipe or quail on toast.

This left our Governor in a fix—not knowing
what to do,
For what he took to be a curse, had proved a
blessing true.
"But yet I may amend," said he, "this error,
though a whopper—
By bidding all to thank the Lord for sending us
the hopper."

CAPTAIN BOB RILEY.

An' so ye never heard that yarn
'Bout ol' Captain Bob—well, I'm durn!
How long have ye been livin' here?
Hain't ye givin' me the queer?
Hones' injin? Waal then say you-
Un's shall heve it an' min' its true.

Bob, he runs in the Anchor Line—
An' hez ever sence fifty-nine,
He's pa'ticlar too, an' talk 'bout style,
O, I guess not! waal, I should smile!
Why, look here, straunger, he's been known
To look at a boat 'n gev her tone.

That wuz Bob fur 'bout twenty year,
Till somehow 'er 'nuther—it wuz queer,
His luck it changed; an' so one trip
He got in a storm that did rip
His chimneys cl'ar off to the deck,
An' dumped 'em overboard a wreck.

She wuz repaired an' left agin,
But struck a gale, an' durn my skin
Ef she didn't come home 'thout her stacks.
Says Bob, "it's chimneys that she lacks."
"Yes," sez the boss, "it seems to me
She's bent on bein' a muly."

Waal, up they hist's another set,
An' farst'nd 'em to stay, ye bet,
When the boss says, "I 'low they'll stay
Till ye git back home, anyway.
So down the river the boat flew,
An' tossin' high smoke, I tell you.

At fus' the weather it wuz fa'r,
An' so Bob, he sets in his chair
On the roof. It's big, fur ye see
Bob weighs two hundred and ninety.
That's jes his size, an' ye can bet
He hain't an' easy man upset.

All went smooth till on the hum run,
When Bob spies a cloud 'n says, "there's fun
Ahead sure, for the ol' storm king
Is comin' for his reg'lar thing,
But I want non' o' it in mine."
An' then he yells, "bring up a line

An' tie me to these here chimneys,
Fur I'm a gwine along with these."
Waal, the next minute 'way they went—
Or at least that wuz their intent—
But when the storm had cleared away,
There sat Bob an' the chimneys—they

Wuz hangin' to the ropes all right—
Not overboard by a durn sight,
Fur they couldn't get 'way with him—
I tell ye Bob's a dandy Jim,
He swore he'd bring them chimneys home
Or lose his job, an' so they come.

AN ODE TO AUTUMN.

   'Tis fall,
   And all
The latest fashions are on tap,
   And female gall
   That comes to pall
Our spirits with that never-ending cry,
Which makes us think it would be sweet to die.

   O life
   And strife,
That rhyme and fit each other passing well;
   O maid and wife,
   O merchant's knife,
That cuts the goods that never are on sale,
And all the things that make us weep and wail.

   Come now
   And vow
To serve us in our hour of need,
   And show us how
   To point our prow
For that fair port on which our thoughts are bent,
Where roosts the winter's coal and monthly rent.

That we
May see
The cheer that autumn ought to bring—
The fat tur-ke,
With cranber-e,
And pumpkin pies of real ancestral size,
And other luxuries that we highly prize.

THE WHISKY RING.

1875.

"All aboard!" the conductor said:
   "Ready!" the engineer replied,
With signals from the engine's head,
   Which fainter grew until they died
     At the city's side.

For, getting steam, the engine lit
   Out up the road, and over space,
As though the very fates spurred it—
   Leading the train a reckless chase
     In that midnight race.

Spanning rivers and piercing hills,
   Threading the woods with golden light;
Anon a screech which caused the quills
   Of waking fowls to stand upright
     In terror and fright.

On to the Capitol they flew—
   Two hundred passengers or more—
The Governor, a dozen or two
   Of Senators, besides a score
     For a house still lower.

They talked of politics and laws,
   Of finance and affairs of State,
The whisky ring, and wagged their jaws
   Long and loud of its terrible fate,
     While they took theirs straight.

"Hunky fellows, well met," you say;
   And so they seemed; but don't be rash—
The State has berths that never pay—
   Pan out neither honor nor cash—
     Why, they ain't worth hash.

Sol in the east rose round and red,
   When all stepped off the pausing train,
The Governor stood and scratched his head—
   "What! members wearing ball and chain?—
     Will you jest explain?"

"'That's all right, Gov'nr"—shaking his hand—
An officer said; "these boys are booked
For the lower house, you understand—
Sent up for taking their whisky crooked.
The Governor *looked!*"

THE NOBLE RED MAN.

Big Moccasin Jim
Was what they called him.
A Winnebago, tall and slim,
Born and brought up way out there
On the Western plains, somewhere—
Where they lift the white man's hair.

"Child of the forest!"
Oh, give us a rest!
A lazy lumex, or I'm blest.
"Ugh!" he grunts, "big Injun me heap!
Fire-water and tobac' cheap,
The great White Father red man keep!"

Well, this Indian—
And it was a sin—
Would loaf about the post and grin,
Waiting for his regular grub,
Nothing abashed by kick or snub—
Total depravity to the hub.

Till the officer said—
Scratching his head
And quoting a line you have read—
"How distance lends enchantment to
And beautifies many a view
A close inspection might look through.

"None of this in mine—
Throwing pearls to swine,
Who tends the grape may drink the wine;
Who sows the seed may reap the grain.
And the 'Prodigal' may not complain
To find the calf already slain.

And he formed a ring,
Which was just the thing
To make the child of the forest sing
"Big Injun no git heap to eat—
Pale-face men muchee Injun cheat."
This was the speech he did repeat.

Wall, so thin he grew—
What I speak is true—
That you might look that Indian through;
The shadow he cast on the ground
Was, on close inspection, found
Caused by the pelt he had around.

But the Government
Got upon the scent,
When a good Friend straightway went
With power to investigate,
And then report unto the state,
Whether he found things crooked or straight.

Well, this old Broadbrim,
All in Quaker trim,
With coat reaching low down on him,
Sought the post, but 'tis inferred,
It wasn't the red man's side he heard,
He left next day with—"mum's the word."

To the State he said,
"Friends, it is bread
And meat which ails the man that's red,
It's plainly evident to me
Civilization don't agree
With the noble aborigenee."

THE MYSTERY OF KERRY PATCH.

There are mysteries in this world that are never
    cleared away,
And will not be understood until the final judg-
    ment day;
But of all the hidden secrets there are few indeed
    can match
The story of the newsboy who lived in "Kerry
    Patch."

He was but a child in years—had seen of birth-
    days only six—
Though the capricious goddess Fortune had
    dealt him many licks;
Every dud upon his body showed where gaping
    rents had been,
And yet rags become respectable when scrupu-
    lously clean.

Every morning, bright and early, he would board
    the passing car,
With his scanty stock in trade, and call out,
    "Papers, here you are!"
Spoke in accents low and feeble, and in a serious
    tone,
As though nursing some great sorrow that he
    wished not to be known.

Men would shake their heads and mutter,
    "Hav'n't any time to read:
Times are hard, and every nickel counts!" Oh,
    miserable creed!
Sympathy is loth to enter where no interest is at
    stake;
And charity, at best, but follows in a business
    wake.

But one day a splendid lady the poor little child
    caressed,
As a mother might her darling, and a dozen
    kisses pressed
Right upon his rosy lips, as she drew him to her
    seat;
Said she really couldn't help it, for he looked so
    nice and sweet.

Then she questioned him of home and spoke a
    kindly word of cheer;
Was he prosperous and happy? But he answered
    with a tear
Dropped upon her silken garment as he struggled
    to be free,
And petulantly muttered: "Oh, please, missus
    let me be!"

In a moment he had vanished—then there came
    a piercing cry,
See the child beneath the wheels of the car that's
    passing by;
"Too late!" men say and shake their heads,
    while women faint away,
Was it carlessness? No matter. Dead, mangled,
    there he lay.

They bore him to the alley, followed by the
    motley crowd,
With his torn and crumpled papers wrapped
    about him as a shroud,
Asking of the ragged urchins that were running
    on before,
Where the little gamin lived, and to please point
    out the door.

"That's his home, right over there in that house
   across the way;
But his mother's very sick—they think she'll
   not live out the day—
Go up gently, if you please, sir, for the noise
   affects her so;
Doctor says it's nearly over—thought this morning she would go."

Silently and sad they entered, paused and gazed
   about the room—
Not a whisper, not an echo—all was silent as the
   tomb.
And they laid the little gamin close beside her
   on the bed;
But she never saw her child, for the mother, too,
   was dead!

That's the mystery of Kerry Patch; and you'll
   think it rather queer,
But it's all was ever known of them by any one
   round here.
Some thought she'd been a lady fallen from her
   high estate;
All declared she was a woman worthy of a better
   fate.

What their history, or secret, the world may never know,
For they searched the room for proof in every corner, high and low;
Neither note nor superscription any evidence revealed—
All was blank, unmeaning, silent, as their graves in "Potter's Field."

NO LUCK IN PRAYER.

It's the wick'd 'z gits the cream down here,
    An' the pius 'z gits the crust,
But the ways o' Providence air queer
    An' I reck'n we'll hev ter trust.

I've alus went on religion some,
    An' I 'low I've done my shar'
To'ards sendin' souls ter kingum come—
    But I ain't no luck in pray'r.

Why when the k'ards went agin me flat,
    An' I los' my bottom red,
An' riz a stake on my boots an' hat,
    What d' you think that I said?

Did I blow an spout an' want ter fight?
    Not much, fur that ain't my trade.
I goes ter my room that very night
    An' got down 'n my knees 'n pray'd.

I tol' the Lo'd how the thing 'd gone,
    An' dwelt on my arful luck,
How Luke hed my yoke o' steers 'n pawn,
    An how arf'ly I war stuck.

Besides he didn't belong ter the chu'ch,
    An' war giv'n ter gain' an' sin,
Tuk pride 'n leavin' saints 'n the lu'ch
    An' ropin' the members in.

Waal, I felt rel'eved an' went ter work,
    Plum full o' relig'ous strength;
Ye see I never war called a shirk,
    An I alus goes my length.

So I staked my trousers on the tray,
    An waited fur Luke ter tu'n,
But he raked em in indiff'rently,
    Like it warn't o' no concern.

No! thar ain't no salvation fur me!
    I hev got no show up thar,
I'm 'umble 'z any one brok' kin be,
    But I ain't no luck in pray'r.

CIVIL RIGHTS IN SHREVEPORT.

There air things in this worl' legislation can't
  reach,
  Questions statesmen do not understand,
Impulses they fail in endeavorin' to teach
  Us to master an' hold in command.

I've no doubt it's correct to pass civil rights laws
  For the colored; but I must request—
An' I do it with all due respect for the cause—
  Don't send 'em to Shreveport to test.

One come to the hotel an' he wrote down his name
  In characters quite dashin' an' bold—
Said the clerk, "You air colored," he replied
    "I'm the same,"
  When their eyes at each other they rolled.

Two o'clock wuz the hour an' the tables wuz spread
  For the guests who now marched in to dine,
When, would you believe it the ol' reprobate said:
  "Hash ready? show me up, I'll hev mine."

The Caucasian waiter drew hisse'f up with pride
   An' then answered, "Ef you know what's well,
You'll make yerse'f scarce here, come now, git
     up and slide
Er you'll dine in a place—I'll not spell."

But he waltzed up the steps which wuz fully two
     flights,
   With his thumbs in the arms o' his vest,
An' aroun' the long hall ez though viewin' the
     sights,
   When he final'y set down with the rest.

Then the women retired to their rooms in disgust,
   An' Si Sanderson said, "Well this lays"—
An' he rose to his feet ez though greatly non-
     plussed—
"Over anything seen in these days."

An' he let fly a ball o' potatoes an' fish,
   Then salads, pickled onions an' pears,
Sullibubs an' jelly, an' so every dish,
   Till they topped off with tables an' chairs.

We tunnelled the wreck an' we found the remains
    Buried under the dining room traps,
But thinkin' a funeral a sheer wastin' o' pains
    Sent 'em out in a basket o' scraps.

There air things in this worl' legislation can't reach,
    Questions statesmen should not agitate,
Ef they will, let 'em slip in a clause, I beseech,
    That will pay for our demolished plates.

THE HERO OF NATCHEZ BEND.

Thar air men ez air sot up ez heroes,
    That don't do much, ye'll allow,
Then agin thar air plenty o' those
    Can't git thar names up no how.

An' a man that runs on the river
    May save more lines 'n enough,
An' s'archin' the papers diskiver
    They ain't even gin him a puff.

Now I don't think this is all reg'lar,
    'Taint treatin' we-uns O. K.
I know, fur ye see I hev been thar,
    An that is what makes me say

That a chap ez does his levelest
    In bringin' an ol' craft through,
An hap'ns ter git jerk'd ter his long rest
    Ain't ter be sneeezed at by you.

Ez war the case with Bagly Harris,
    Who froze ter the Creole's wheel,
Fur he seed his duty ez clear ez
    Daylight, an' he didn't squeal.

Though he never knowed the prevailin'
    Storm hed scooped him overboard,
An' the pilot house war a sailin'
    Along o' its own accord.

He tried fur ter blow on the whistle
    An' holler down ter the bar,
Ter his ol' friend big Sandy Bissell
    Ter send him a drink up thar.

Fur he wusn't awar' that the Creole
    War safely tied ter a tree,
An' the capt'in an' every soul
    Asleep ez sound ez could be.

So he held her level an' steady
    In the boilin' water 'n wind,
An' keeping a lookout ahead, he
    Expected soon fur ter find

The bank, so's he could make a landin'.
   But he never found the shor'
An' all through the night he kept standin'
   An' steerin' jes ez afor'.

When they foun' him he war still clingin'
   With his teeth unter the wheel,
Jes ez though he hed bin a bringin'
   Through a craft ez hed a keel.

But col' in death's embrace, an' grim—
   Ter Canaan's lan' he crossed,
An' I hope the angels won't tell him
   He war the unly one lost.

Thar's men ez air sot up ez heroes,
   That don't do much, ye'll allow,
Then agin thar air plenty o' those
   Ez can't git thar names up no how.

An' so it war with Bagly Harris,
   Who war made o' the true stuff,
An' I reckon it unly fa'r is
   Ter gin the ol' man a puff.

THE APPLE MAID.

'Twas in that lovely season of the year
    When pawpaws ripen and grow soft and black,
And in the daily market do appear
    To tempt loose change from the depleted sack,
        That Sally Skinner, the fair apple maid,
        With ladened basket to the levee strayed.

She was quite young, just bordering on sixteen,
    Of comely presence as you'd wish to see,
Although she wasn't dressed just like a queen
    (Her dress flapped in the wind a little free);
        But she was lively, and could sell more fruit
        Than all the peddlers on the creek to boot.

Her mother took in washing on the hill,—
    Sometimes took something stronger in, 'twas said;
But then she was a woman of strong will,
    And never let it run off with her head,
        But plied her business in an even way,
        And earned her daily bread from day to day.

And so they prospered, as 'tis plain all should
    Who pass their time away in doing good,
And in due time financially took rank
    As having quite a nest-egg in the bank;
        But lovely Juliet met her Romeo,
        And why should Sally ever unloved go?

He was deck-sweeper on the Mary Ann,
    A youth of gallous stride and coarse red hair—
Would soon grow up to be a bully man;
    He now could chew tobacco, fight and swear;
        How could the lovely creature answer nay,
        To "Sally, pass the produce up this way?"

It charmed the girl to see her lover eat;
    And so she gazed, and never once mistrusted,
While he was taking in the sour and sweet,
    That he or she, or both, would soon be busted;
        But so it was, for when she homeward strayed,
        She found her fruit, her time and money
            played.

The empty basket made her mother smile,
    For it did argue a most prosperous day;
But when she said: "Dear Sally, where's your
        pile?"

The maiden turned her head another way.
   You may imagine, but I can't express,
   How old dame Skinner did her offspring bless.

But women are but women after all;
   And when the bankrupt daughter did explain,—
Although denouncing her commercial fall,—
   Resolved at once to set up trade again.
     So, swiftly to the bank the mother went,
     And, check in hand, demanded her last cent.

Then, calling Sally to her side, she said:
   "Go buy a peck, and try your luck again;
But shun the fellow with the sandy head,
   Or from this house forever you'll remain."
     And so she sallied forth, and talked and smiled,
     And sought the youth again, the silly child.

She found him brushing up the lower deck,
   But meeting, they both did sit down to rest;
He of her apple cart soon made a wreck,
   And left the girl again sorely distressed,
     Who gazed on him and then looked in the basket;
     How dear he was we scarcely need to ask it.

They married, and were happy in their love;
    Promotion came and raised him to deck hand—
And on the raging creek he still does rove,
    While she's sole owner of an apple stand.
        My story's brief, but long enough to prove
        The world's still running in the same old
            groove.

THE COUNTY FAIR.

Waal, yes, ye see, 'at we're on han',
   An' anxious fur to do our shar',
Fur o' all 'mus'ents, un'erstan',
   Me an' Merlindy prefer the Fa'r.

These air the curiosities
   A man don't tire o' lookin' at—
Suthin' ter help pay taxes
   An' keep things goin' 'n sech ez that.

Cows ez 'll gev a pail o' milk,
   An' bred 'till they 'pear half human,
An' hosses' 'at shine jes like silk,
   An' run—ef ye'll wait ol' 'oman,

An' ta'k a spell ter Deacon Wells,
   I'll try'n pick a winner er two,
An' te'ch some o' them city swells
   What a plain country chap kin do.

Want ter go long, eh! an' not wait—
   Wimin' they say aint much fur luck,
But mar'd men mus' b'ar thar fate—
   That gal war bo'n in ol' Kentuck.

CHRISTMAS EVE.

He bears rich jewels to his lady's bower,
    And pockets Santa-Claus-wise filled with toys;
    Love tokens that forecast the morrow's joys,
When merry bells ring out the welcome hour.

Happy the home that knows such scenes as these,
    Where loving hands arrange each glad surprise,
    Keeping alive the hallowed memories
That came to us from out the centuries.

THE SAD FATE OF PETER JONES.

Once, in the flight of time, there lived a boy
   Who came of poor but honest parentage;
He was his mother's pet and father's joy,
   And just exactly eighteen years of age
     When he did quit this sublunary sphere,
     And died a hero, as it will appear.

He was an unsophisticated youth,
   From the verdant fields of Posey County,
Who never could speak anything but truth,
   Though offered for each falsehood a large
      bounty;
     And when he came to town to seek a living,
     Much good advice to other boys kept giving.

He never played with marbles or with balls,
   And saw no good in any of these ways,
But loved to view the horses in their stalls,
   And this one criticise and that one praise;
     And daily made commendable progression
     In studying for the bob-tail car profession.

For many weeks he strolled about the city,
   And ran in debt for board and all expenses;
He made some friends, who said it was a pity,
   And vowed the boy was losing all his senses—
     For he would stand for hours, with his mouth ajar,
    And view with ecstacy each passing car.

One day he got a driver's situation,
   And felt, at length, that he had drawn a prize;
In fact, it was an active occupation,
   In which a youth was very apt to rise—
     Fur every one who did engage to drive
     Was bound by contract to get up at five.

He took the reins as one ordained to rule,
   Then tightened them a little with each hand,
As though to say, "Well, now, good Mister Mule,
   Hereafter I would have you understand
     That when I say to you, 'Come, go alang,'
     That I am captain of this 'ere shebang."

Just then the starter blew a piercing blast,
   Which made the animal prick up its ears
And dash ahead at gait so very fast

As to arouse in Peter Jones some fears;
   But when the car began to jolt and shake,
   The inmates hallooed out, "Put down the brake!"

Instead of putting down, he screwed it up,
   Which only made the mule rush onward faster;
When, lo! the car run on a big pull pup,
   And Peter whispered to himself, "Dod blast her!"
   But, after going on one wheel awhile,
   It settled down again in splendid style;

Then dashed ahead at a terrific rate,
   Alike unheeding rings to stop or hail.
The passengers were in a fearful state—
   Strong men did pray and weaker women wail;
   Spectators said the sight was truly grand
   To witness Peter drive that "one in hand."

Just then another car came round the curve—
   Two single mules were blended into one;
Ask for those passengers! I would observe
   That "they have put their angel plumage on;"
   And in the wreck were found the cold remains
   Of Peter Jones, still holding to the reins.

The coroner was summoned to the scene,
   And held an inquest on the men and mules.
He said the accident might not have been
     Had both the cars observed the comp'ny's rules,
       Which read emphatically, in white and black;
      "Two cars shall never pass upon one track."

MISSISSIPPI SMITHERS.

"Hello! elev'n—waal, let it strike;
   Kem, Frazier, kem—a song!
Simpson, thar. an' Marlinspike,
   Jes pass the grog along.
We'll cut fur deal—the highest k'ard—"
   Says a voice from the draught they sip:
"Dark the river rolls below"—
   "Well, durn it, let her rip."

"Converse made an awful smoke,
   With that air J. M. White;
I reckon that the catfish woke
   When that craft kem in sight.
But Lor', she's gone an' hed her day;
   Her famous job is done—"
"Dark the river rolls below—"
   "Well, durn it, let it run."

"Fifty year ago to-night—
   Drink, boys, I'm gettin' dry—
The Swiftsure went up like a kite;
   You orto've seen us fly.
She'd pass'd the Homer under way,
   But the critter busted wide—"
"Dark the river rolls below"—
   "Well, durn it, let her slide."

"Smith war planted in the field,
   Above the mouth of cache;
An' Oakes hasn't, sence she squealed,
   Tuk up the pan fur hash.
An' Sally Smithers—waal,
   I've been 'lone fur many a year,"
"Dark the river runs below"—
   "How strange the lights appear."

"Waal, yes, them were the palmy days!
   At least, that's what they say;
Fur blessin's here we seldom praise
   Until they're pass'd away.
But Sallie—she went long ago;
   How peartly time has flew!
"Ho! Broadus, catch Old Smithers! thar—
   He's quit the river, too."

A MUD THEORY.

'Tis a theory of the schools,
   The earth was once a fluid,
And growing solid as it cools,
   Will yet become imbued
With such a quantity of cold,
As not a living thing to hold.

That is, the sun's not all the heat
   That nourishes vegetation.
For while Sol warms the head, the feet
   Draw from the incrustation—
The vegetables' feet I mean—
Sufficient warmth to keep them green.

Well, be this as it may elsewhere —
   I speak but for this section—
And grieve to say I cannot share
   My thoughts in this connection;
'Tis true, or I'm an arrant sinner,
Terra firma here gets daily "thinner."

SANDY POSEY.

Thar's signs ez goes back on the ol'est man,
    Thar's clouds ez never brings rain,
Signs ez air apt ter mislead,
    Deceptions ez causes pain.
An the bes' that we kin do ol' Satan
    'Ill now an' then make a gain:
    Fur instance, I'll jes explain.

Ez in the case o' big Sandy Posey,
    At the ol' camp-meetin' groun',
He hed every symptom
    O' hevin' salvation foun'.
An' right in the middle o' the sermon
    Commenced jumpin' up an down
    An' then ter rollin aroun'.

I felt sartin ez it war a cl'ar case
    O' the spirit-movin power
That he'd got a holt o' him,
    Then an' thar that very hour;
Fur the ol' sinner shook till his dice box
    An' k'ards fell in a shower,
    He hed drap'd his las' bower.

Then he looked up inter the apple trees
    An' inquired, "who kin it be
A roustin' up thar in that fork
    Ez done this hyar thing ter me?"
An I said, "Thank the Lo'd, man,
    Fur causin' ye fur ter see"—
    Still a lookin' up a tree.

"Waal, yes, I'm seein' some now, ol' pardner,
    An' I wish that ye would try
An' fin' out the on'ry scamp
    Ez squirted inter my eye
That air terbac'er juice;" this surprised me,
    So 'at I made no reply:
    Fac' ez 'at I didn't try.

Thar's signs ez goes bac' on the ol'est man,
    Thar's clouds ez never brings rain;
Signs ez air apt ter mislead,
    Deceptions ez causes pain.
Ez in the case o' big Sandy Posey
    Who 'ill not fool me soon ag'in,
    Ez 'bout my way o' thinkin'.

THE NEW AMAZONS.

Say have you heard of great Dio*
And his female brigade in Ohio?
    The charge that they made
    On King Alcohol's trade,
Opened that Old Monarch's eye, O.

When Peter the Hermit first made his
Crusade 'gainst those demons of Hades,
    'Twas an awful mistake
    Those warriors to take
Instead of an army of ladies.

For had those uncivilized nations,
With all their unfriendly relations,
    Been besieged with such charms,
    They'd have thrown down their arms—
Gone back on their chief and their rations.

*Dio Lewis.

Then sing us no more songs of Bacchus,
And cease with your nonsense to rack us;
  We will cheerfully flee
  From the joys of a spree,
If the women will only attack us.

So, forward, brigade of Ohio,
Led on by redoubtable Dio;
  The aroma which slips
  From thy warriors' sweet lips
Is better than any old rye, O.

SANDY THOMPSON'S STEERS.

Waal, I ain't much on spinnin' yarns,
    An' tellin' jokes an' sich,
Fur I git things all mixed up,
    Can't tell t'other frum which.
But I s'pose ye'r, boun' ter hear it,
    So draw aroun' yer cheers,
An' I'll tell ye 'bout my scrape
    With Sandy Thompson's steers.

I'd been a haulin' o' some logs
    An' jes unhitched a pull —
When the hook got cotched in my boot,
    An' jerked me agin ol' bull,
Which made the steers skedaddle
    An' foot it through the snow,
An' they kept a goin' faster
    The mor' I holler'd whoa.

They snaked me down through the cl'arin',
   An' struck the ol' turnpike,
An I 'low it's safe ter say
   Ye never saw the like.
They puffed an' blowed an made more fuss
   Than a Mississippi craf',
That war a makin' raillroad time
   With a barge in tow back af'.

We pass'd good De'con Sanford's house
   Ez he war hevin' pra'r,
An' the houn's they yelped an' start'd
   Ez ef Ol' Nick war thar.
The good exhorter heard the noise,
   But lowed they'd struck a trail,
An' kep' on prayin jes ez though
   It warn't o' no avail.

I brought up stradle o' a stump,
   But the team rushed along
Like a locomotive engine
   With the steam tu'ned on strong.
An' my boot went jumpin' arter—
   I never shell furgit,
Waal, I rec'on them air critters
   Air hollin' o' it yit.

They say that all is fur the bes',
    Hed we the power ter see,
But thar air things in this hyar worl'
    That air myst'ries ter me.
An' the mor' I stedy on it
    The mor' it still appears,
That no good could ever kem
    O' that on'ry yoke o' steers.

THE UNRECONSTRUCTED.

Sandy Hawkins war his name, an' he resided down in Pike,
An' fur railin' on the Yankees no one ever saw his like.
He'd cuss 'em with an eloquence so extremely rich an rar',
It partuk o' all the earnestness an' fe'vency o' pra'r.

"A carpet bagger," he would say, with his peculiar sneer,
"Is not the style o' citizen 'll fin' it healthy hyar."
An' then ef any war aroun' jes ter tech em ter the quick,
He'd declar' he never yit hed seed a Yank he couldn't lick.

He'd bluffed off all new comers, while a number
　　he had whaled,
An 'them ez he hedn't pummeled he'd effectually
　　quailed.
Till one day he struck a straunger, an' in con-
　　versation with
The same, he soon discovered that his name, it
　　war Jim Smith.

They'd played a game o' poker, which war
　　quarter-ante straight,
But the k'ards went back on Sandy at a fearful
　　rapid rate.
Till the whol' 'mount o' currency that hed be-
　　longed ter him
War snugly rustercatin' in the panterloons o'
　　Jim.

Then he 'lowed how he'd been cheated, an' his
　　dander ris an' ris,
While he continered ter express the feelings that
　　war his—
Said 'twar nigger luck ez beat him, an' warn't
　　done 'pon the square,
An' 'twar evident he meant ter go fur Jim right
　　then an' thar.

But Mr. Smith war peaceful, an' not so easily beguiled,
An' he stood an' looked at Sandy ez though pained ter see him riled,
'Lowed he didn't keer ter fight a man fur sech a trivial cause,
An' besides it warn't proper thus ter trespass on the laws.

Is thar reason in a mad man, or infuriated steer,
Or a hoss when he imagin's su'thin's wrong about the gear.
Or a Mississippi craft that hez made up her mind ter bust,
Or the bank whar ye deposit when ye call ter ast fur trust?

'Twar 'about this way with Sandy, who struck out lef' an right,
An' swore he'd hev his money back or else he'd hev a fight.
So they got inter a tussle which lasted fur quite a spell,
An' when the thing war over Sandy didn't feel so well.

They picked him up an' bore him *hors de combat*
    frum the ground,
An' filled him full o' licker, 'lowin that mought
    bring him roun'.
Fur a moment breath kem ter him an' he looked
    'roun' 'n' sighed
"We air ruined by the Yanks," an' he closed
    his lips an' died.

THE WHITE COLLAR LINE.

Bill come into the trade with the durndes' ol' craf',
She wuz broke down amidship an' hogged all abaf'.
An' her chimneys, they leaned at right angles away,
But he'd writ on her wheelhouse, "I've come here to stay."
The people all laughed at that air plug o' a boat,
An' declar'd that her capt'in should hev a new coat:
Fur his elbows wuz out an' his knees wuzn't in,
But when a man's hones' his rags ain't no sin.

He wuz deck han' an' rouster—stood watch at the wheel,
An' would fire till he made the safety valve squeal.

Waal, the berths that he hel' I 'low wuzn't a
    few,
Fur the boys all declar'd he wuz chambermaid,
    too.
He would run any craf' in the trade out o' sight,
An' wuz never foun' nappin' in day time or
    night,
But would land fur a hail jes to take in a dime,
An' the people, they said, "gev us Bill every
    time."

The other boats a'lowed that the thing it wuz
    plain
That their business wuz played ef this chap did
    remain;
So to put up a job they straightway went about,
The object o' which wuz jist to raise William
    out.
They cut down on the rates, an tuk passengers
    cheap:
What before they'd charged one, now would pay
    fur a heap.
But Bill stayed in the game with his deuces
    an' trays,
An' what worried 'em most, he kept standin' the
    raise.

Competition went on, an the money it flew;
When they landed fer freight Bill wuz alus thar, too,
An' rak'd in such a shar' o' the trade which they sought
That they swore by the pow'rs "'twuz a tartar they'd caught."
Yes, he stayed, you bet, and you will find him there yit;
He will tell you about all the fights that he's fit—
Fur Bill he wuz game, an attended to biz;
An you see all them *white collared boats?*— waal, they're his.

BLANNERHASSETT'S.

"Blannerhassett's?" said the Captain: "that's
    it, there.
But this bar's rather shallow—Sykes, the lead!
Seven and a quarter? well, that's fair;
    But hold her level, Birch, there's rocks
        ahead—
Ah! there you are, now let her go along,
And tell the engineer to work her strong.

"Well, all I know about the island is:
    Just previous to the year eighteen hundred,
Blannerhassett and that wife of his
    Settled here. The neighbors said they blun-
        dered,
And vowed no feller with sech soft white hands
Would ever make much headway cl'arin' lands.

"But he had what the people wanted—gold!
   Which is a power, you know, of some dimen-
      sions;
And all he had to do, so I am told,
   Was just to hint at what were his intentions—
Whether to clear a field or bridge a run—
It wasn't no time till the job was done.

"And soon they rigged the island up so fine,
   It seemed a jewel risen from the water.
Of all the farms this one did take the shine;
   Folks came to see it from every quarter.
The rare flowers, plants, fruits and shrubbery,
They say, was really a sight to see.

"As to his wife, why, I've heard them tell
   About her beauty, and how she played
On the harp and piano till the swell
   Of music out on the waters strayed,
And charmed a boat's crew that was floatin' by,
Till Sandy Jones forgot that he held high.

"And how they come to quit the place, eh! O!
   You see, a certain chap from New York city,
Who came a coasting down the river slow—
   I know you'll say it was a pity
That he should stop at this here paradise,
   Where everything was goin' on so nice.

"But Aaron Burr did stop—that was his name—
   And him and Blannerhassett had a chat,
In which Mr. Burr did talk of fame,
   And power, and empire, ermine, and all that,
Till Blannerhassett got so badly stuck
That he concluded just to try his luck.

"And that is all—he never did come back,
   For years the madam pined, till, broken-
      hearted,
She died; and so the island went to rack,
   And it's now, you see, about where it started.
The weeds are rather thrifty, you'll allow,
And that old house ain't quite a palace now."

www.ingramcontent.com/pod-product-compliance
Lightning Source LLC
Chambersburg PA
CBHW020823230426
43666CB00007B/1082